Racism, W[...] Your Sting?

A provocative look at the beginning and the end of racism

Eric Tangumonkem, Ph.D.

IEM PRESS (PO Box 831001, Richardson, TX 75080) functions only as a book publisher. As such, the ultimate design, content, editorial accuracy, and views expressed or implied in this work are those of the author. No part of this publication may be reproduced, stored in a retrieval system, or transmitted in any way by any means— electronic, mechanical, photocopy, recording, or otherwise—without the prior permission of the copyright holder, except as provided by USA copyright law. Unless otherwise noted, all Scriptures are taken from the Holy Bible, New International Version®, NIV®. Copyright © 1973, 1978, 1984, 2011 by Biblica, Inc.™ Used by permission of Zondervan. All rights reserved worldwide. www. zondervan.com

ISBN 10: 1-947662-57-0
ISBN 13: 978-1-947662-57-5

Library of Congress Catalog Card Number: 2019950466

Table of Contents

Foreword v

Introduction 1

Chapter 1: The Beginning of Racism 7

Chapter 2: The Complex Interplay of Superiority
and Inferiority... 31

Chapter 3: Telling It Like It Is 51

Chapter 4: Lessons from the Past 65

Chapter 5: The Way Forward 91

Chapter 6: The End of Racism 101

Chapter 7: The Banishment of Racism Now and Forever 111

Acknowledgment 119

About the Author 121

Foreword

D r. Eric Tangumonkem is my nephew. When he was an undergraduate student at the university, he visited me regularly. I saw in him a young man who is physically, intellectually, spiritually, and aesthetically well endowed. He moves with passion, positive inquisitiveness, vision, and magnanimity of heart.

Eric is also a prolific writer. It does not surprise me that he has written about racism. He sees this sensitive, controversial, and perennial topic as a social construct and an absurdity. This is because it has no scientific basis. Consequently, it should be renounced by its actual and potential originators and promoters.

Being a child of God, the Almighty Creator, Eric views racism as a monster that has brought devastation to humanity. This book clearly explains that racism is a result of fear, ignorance, greed, selfishness, and discrimination on the basis of ethnic group, skin color, culture, religion, sex, education, economic and social class. Furthermore, there are factors that fan racism, such as the unpredictable or unfamiliar.

We are all human beings created equal in God's image, though unique or not the same. We have the same blood running through our veins. There is, therefore, one human race. The varying skin pigmentations ought not to be considered a stigma, but a portrayal of the artistic ingenuity of the Creator God. Variety should be considered and celebrated as the spice of life.

Eric makes it clear that what has brought about and sustained racism or discrimination among human beings is the depravity of the human heart since from the inception of humanity, due to man's disobedience in the Garden of Eden. Humanity disconnected with his Creator and his heart, which ought to pour out love, becomes depraved. Such a heart fuels racism with anger, bitterness, resentment, hatred. egoism, bigotry, covetousness, avarice, lies, wickedness, just to cite some.

This book is a must-read because of its inspiring and edifying nature. It is for all who want to be better human beings, in order to build a better harmonious global village as compared to the chaotic one we have today.

Rev. Prof. Lekunze, Edward Forcha
Former Dean, Secretary General, Vice Rector
Protestant University of Central Africa

Introduction

A lot of ink has already been spilled on paper regarding the subject of racism, but the issue seems to be as stubborn as a granite mountain that resists any attempts to be broken down by agents of weathering and mass wasting. While many governments and communities have passed legislation to tame this "monster," it somehow finds a way to raise its ugly head and stare mockingly at us. Each time the issue of racism is mentioned, tensions are high, reason is thrown out the window and replaced by an emotional outburst that only makes the situation worse.

If you doubt the gravity of this situation, all you need to do is to Google the word "racism". I did and I found about 253,000,000 results (0.32 seconds). Lord, have mercy. We are in the 21st century and have made a lot of advances in technology, medicine, communication, artificial intelligence, and many other areas, but it seems we are having a lot of difficulties eradicating racism.

When you turn on the news, especially in the United States of America, a day does not go by without you hearing somebody being labeled a racist. The situation has deteriorated since Donald Trump became the president. A day does not go by without somebody calling him a racist. You may be saying that he is a racist and the racist-in-chief, as some have decided to label him. But is he? What about the accusation that all who elected him are racists? Are we saying that racism is no longer about the color of somebody's skin, but between the Democrats and the Republicans? It seems racism has morphed into a new monster that has taken over the Republican party. If you are a Republican, no matter who you are, this monster has polluted you and you are now a racist. Meanwhile, the minority-loving, protective, and

1

caring Democratic Party has somehow cleansed and sanitized itself of this vile monster. Therefore, all who identify with the Democratic Party are not racists, but inclusive, tolerant, accepting, and loving of all people.

The question is why is racism such a charged word? Why do the politicians like to talk about it a lot? Why is it that after the United States of America elected the first biracial president, racism is still the top item on the news? I have deliberately mentioned that President Barack Obama was biracial because his mother was white and his father was a black man from Kenya. These days, words seem to have multiple meanings, and the main actors behind mass media are the spin doctors who insist on setting the narrative that all of us must follow. President Obama identified himself as a black person, and I do not fault him for that, but the underlying composition of his DNA and who he is does not change. He is biracial, and it is a part of him that cannot be discarded. That said, his election was supposed to be a high point in the life of a country and the world that has had its fair share of racial tensions because of discrimination, slavery, subjugation, lynchings, murders, and all sorts of atrocities. Unfortunately, it seems the issue of racism is getting worse with each passing day. Is this the case?

The purpose of writing this book is to offer a simple solution to this apparent complex problem of racism. There is no attempt here to deny its monstrosity and the havoc and carnage it has caused and is still causing all over the world. Nobody in their right mind can deny the existence of racism and the harm it causes. Are we at the mercy of this monster forever or is there a way out?

While some, in the name of awareness, keep stoking the fires of racism, I will be using an entirely different approach to address this vexing issue that has plagued the human race for thousands of years. Racism and discrimination did not start with the arrival of slaves on the shores of the new world, nor did it start when these slaves were caught and sold by people who looked like them. We need to go past all the great civilizations that practiced this evil and go back to the very beginning when humans were created. If we want to offer any reasonable solution, it is imperative that we go to the source of the problem. Throughout human history, racism has been practiced at varying degrees by different societies at different times.

Before one can make any attempt to provide any lasting solution, it will be important to expand the definition of racism to encompass other forms of discrimination that exist among all humans, no matter where you find them. Take, for example, tribalism and ethnocentric discrimination. While some will argue that there is a big difference between racism, tribalism, and ethnocentrism, I will be arguing here that there is a great commonality among them because the focus is going to be on what drives these three behaviors.

The bottom line is that by default, all humans can discriminate against other people who do not look, speak, eat, believe, and dress like them. In other words, the propensity to be racist exists in all of us. This does not mean that there is a racist gene, but based on how we were raised and nurtured, we tend to seek for "our own" unless taught otherwise. This discrimination becomes problematic when it perpetuated at the expense of other people. Although there is no scientific basis for dividing the human race into different races based on skin color or other factors, this idea of racism still persists because humans like to discriminate. We generally like what is predictable, familiar, and comfortable. Therefore, when we see something new and strange, fear pushes us to want to be protective of our stuff. For us to keep expanding and occupy space, we sow fear in the hearts of other people by creating the illusion of superiority.

This book is going to be addressing this fear-driven superiority and inferiority complex interaction between humans that keeps fueling tribalism, racism, and other forms of discrimination that are detrimental to us living together in peace and harmony.

While there is a great need for legislation to curb these excesses, one will be living in denial if the role of changing one human heart after the other is underlooked. One would have assumed that in the US, with all the laws in the books, the society will be more homogeneous and segregation will be a thing of the past. But the reality on the ground is far from this. You still have churches that are 100% black, white, Latino, and even neighborhoods that are strictly divided into racial lines. The reason is that people have found "clever" ways of circumventing the laws and doing what humans do: discriminate.

Therefore, this book will be speaking directly to the individual and what each one of us can do within our power and sphere of influence to put an end to racism. While it is important to march on the streets and demonstrate and ask for all people to be treated equally and with dignity and respect, it is more effective and productive when each individual becomes the change they desire to see in the world.

This is a personal call for you to start changing because you can only change yourself. You can try to change others, but you will fail. Therefore, if all of us are working on how to change ourselves, at the end of the day, we will all become changed individuals. Our society and our world will change.

As much as this may sound somewhat idealistic, it is a far better alternative to the present approach that is perpetuated by the mass media. It insists that some are the victors while victims are being abused, killed with impunity and incarcerated en mass without cause. You will seldom hear the media talking about positive examples of harmony between blacks and whites, Hispanics and other people. But when a black male is shot dead, they keep feeding the narrative that perpetuates this culture of victimhood and helplessness.

All is not lost! We are not at the mercy of what is fed to us through the media. We can learn to live together by getting to know each other. Forgiveness is not the denial of evil, it is the choice to take the high road that brings healing, hope, and restoration. The strong are those that forgive; the weak live in hatred and allow it to destroy their lives. Nothing negatively impacts and enslaves the human soul like unforgiveness. No wonder the Lord Jesus Christ himself instructed us to forgive 70 times 7 times a day. The instruction does not hinge on us counting the number of times we forgive in a day, but it is saying implicitly that our capacity to forgive should be limitless. Unfortunately, the temptation to want to repay and be vengeful is so strong that we end up drinking the very venom that we wanted those who have hurt us to drink.

The heart of this book is focused on the key elements that make racism possible and how to starve the lifeblood to these key elements and eradicate them from the root. Since racism is based on the faulty notion that one race is superior to another, you need somebody who believes that they are superior and another person who believes that they are inferior. When these two people interact, the outcome will reflect what they believe about themselves and their circumstances. This may sound too simplistic, but it is one of the major drivers of racism. In addition to superiority and inferiority beliefs, acts of impunity and unforgiveness are the other drivers. You have those that believe they are superior, and in their zeal to impose their superiority, they harm those they are trying to keep in their inferior position. The individuals who are hurt "rightly" want to seek revenge and unfortunately fall into the unforgiveness pit, where they become trapped by hate and vengeance.

I hope that the simple message of hope in this book will shed some much-needed light in the darkness of one of the darkest pages of human history. We are going to be affirming that there is one human race. In addition to one human family, none is superior to another, and none is inferior as well. We are all created in the image and likeness of God, and the amount of melanin in our skin does not and should never be used to define us. When we gain this understanding, believe and start acting on it, it is only then that we can all ask the question, "Oh, racism, where is your sting?

Chapter 1:
The Beginning of Racism

Parents and schools should place great emphasis on the idea that it is all right to be different. Racism and all the other 'isms' grow from primitive tribalism, the instinctive hostility against those of another tribe, race, religion, nationality, class or whatever. You are a lucky child if your parents taught you to accept diversity.
Roger Ebert

It has often been said that if we fail to understand history, we are doomed to repeat it. Nothing is truer to this than in the area of racism, because racism has been part of human history for thousands of years now. Although some may erroneously try to make it feel as if racism is a fairly new concept. *In the past, the term racism was not used to refer to the manifestation of this evil behavior.* I am calling racism evil because anything that distorts that which God has called good is trying to corrupt what God has made. The only appropriate word for such an action is evil.

While there are a thousand different ways to approach this subject of racism, tribalism, and ethnocentrism, I have chosen a more holistic approach that will incorporate both the physical and spiritual components of this issue. *I am going to be using the term racism in a more encompassing and broader fashion to include all the tendencies of superiority and inferiority complexes that are driven by fear and propagated by fear.*

Before I get into the definition of terms, it is important to have a baseline. Without establishing a zero point, we will never know if we have made any progress or not. I believe that we are not a result of some cosmic accident because believing that we are a result of an accident and are just living by the dictates of our instincts, it will be difficult for us to see any reason why we should not follow our instincts and discriminate against other people. Nothing will prevent us from taking advantage of other people as long as it guarantees that we move ahead. In other words, if all that we are here to do is to pass our genes to the next generation, then all this talk about racism and being able to live together in harmony and love is baseless. *If survival is all that we are engineered to do, then everything else must be sacrificed on the altar of survival, including love for one another.*

On the contrary, I am of the school of thought that mankind was created and each one of us has a unique purpose. Without a firm understanding of this foundational truth, it is almost impossible to grapple with racial issues, much less come up with workable solutions.

Created in God's image

Let us go back before there were any humans on earth — the time when there were no Black, White, Hispanic, Asian, Aboriginal, American Indians, Indians, etc. In the beginning, after God had created the entire universe and the earth, a decision was made by God himself to create mankind.

Then God said, **"Let us make mankind in our image, in our likeness***, so that they may rule over the fish in the sea and the birds in the sky, over the livestock and all the wild animals, and over all the creatures that move along the ground." Genesis 1:26 New International Version (NIV)*

I have bolded the first part of the verse to emphasize that nobody is an accident because God himself decided out of His free will that the human race be created. One special aspect of the human race is that humans were created in the image of God. We are not an accident and were never intended to be because God did not only propose that we be created, He actually went ahead and created us as the following verse says:

> *So God created mankind in his own image,*
> *in the image of God he created them;*
> *male and female he created them. Genesis 1:27 (NIV)*

All humankind, both male and female, has the image of God stamped on them, so to speak. We are not just flesh and blood moving around without hope and purpose. *We have the image of God and should look at all other people from this understanding.*

After God created male and female in His image, He did not just allow them to roam the earth aimlessly and without purpose. The following verse clearly stipulates what mankind is supposed to be doing:

> *God blessed them and said to them, "Be fruitful and increase in number; fill the earth and subdue it. Rule over the fish in the sea and the birds in the sky and over every living creature that moves on the ground." Genesis 1:28 (NIV)*

It is important to note that after God created mankind, He blessed them before giving them an assignment because He knew that they needed this blessing to be effective in carrying out their assignment successfully. The other thing to note here is that mankind was given the dominion to rule over the entire creation, but not over each other.

This perfect picture of harmony, tranquility, and blessing will soon be perturbed and with it came death, decay, and all the misery and suffering the world is facing right now.

The first broken relationship

After God had finished creating the first man and woman, He placed them in the Garden of Eden, and there was perfect harmony and fellowship between God and humankind. In addition to the harmony between God and the first humans, there was peace and harmony between the first man and woman. God, out of His foreknowledge and deep love for the well-being of Adam and Eve, gave them special instructions on how to conduct themselves in the garden. Out of all the trees in the garden, there was one tree that they were not allowed to eat the fruit, but they could eat the fruits from all the other trees.

As time went on, it seems they got a little distracted. One day, the devil showed up and tempted the woman, who decided to act contrary to the clear instructions that God had given them. She was not forced to disobey God's command, but it is written that

When the woman saw that the fruit of the tree was good for food and pleasing to the eye, and also desirable for gaining wisdom, she took some and ate it. She also gave some to her husband, who was with her, and he ate it. Then the eyes of both of them were opened, and they realized they were naked; so they sewed fig leaves together and made coverings for themselves. Genesis 3:6-7 (NIV)

The woman saw the fruit before the thought of eating it came into her mind. In order words, her eyes acted as a window through which her mind was influenced. Immediately after the pictures of this fruit hit her mind, she started salivating and imagining how well the fruit will taste and how she was going to gain the knowledge of good and evil. All these things transpired in her mind before she picked up the fruit and ate it. There was something sinister that had triggered all these activities: the words that the devil whispered in her ear. "Woman, do not believe what God is telling you. He is preventing you from becoming like Him. If you eat this fruit, you will not die, you will become God."

Corruption of the senses

The five physical senses of vision, hearing, smell, taste, and touch have been given to us to enjoy the physical environment, but they are the pathway to our minds and eventually, our subconscious minds. We are our thoughts because any information that gets into our minds through these senses influences what we believe. *What we believe determines our actions, and our actions determine the outcome of our lives.* These five senses are neutral, but can be used for wrong purposes as we are going to see.

It is sad that Eve allowed her ears to influence her eyes and her eyes to influence her thoughts and her thoughts to influence her actions. What would have happened if Eve refused to listen to the devil? Her eyes would not have strayed. What would have happened if after she listened to the devil and she refused to let her eyes lead her? She would not have seen the fruit, and without seeing the fruit, she would not have thought about how good the fruit will taste. Without her thinking about how delicious the fruit will be if eaten, she would not have picked it up and eaten it.

When Eve ate the forbidden fruit and gave part of it to Adam to eat, their action was the moment the physical senses became corrupt and have since been subjected to this fallen state. Immediately after Adam eats the fruit, both of them realized that they were naked and became ashamed, so they hid. Before their act of disobedience, their eyes did not see any nakedness, even though they were naked, and there was no shame in their hearts. All this changed when they disobeyed God.

God had intended the five senses to be used to enjoy the beauty and abundance in the garden, but Adam and Eve, through their act of disobedience, had corrupted the senses because they allowed their senses to be used to do something that God had strictly forbidden them to do.

The consequences of corrupting the senses

Before Adam and Eve ate the forbidden fruit, there was harmony between them and there was harmony between God and them. There was no fear and no shame, but everything changed immediately after they ate the forbidden fruit. The most significant change was the spiritual death experienced by Adam and Eve. Death is simply a separation, in this case, there was a separation between God and Adam and Eve. This spiritual death resulted from this original sin that Adam and Eve committed.

The original sin also brought with it physical death, pain, decay, and disruption of the harmony between humankind and between God and humankind. The manifestation of this havoc caused by this first act of disobedience is seen in every society and has been part of the human experience for thousands of years.

This implies that all humankind has the propensity to discriminate and to be racist if not checked. Until we start looking at racism from this vantage point, we will be chasing our tails trying to solve a problem that has eluded humankind for millennia. Many may make us feel that the American experience, or the Holocaust in Germany or the transatlantic slave trade or genocide in Rwanda or the murder of millions by the Khmer Rouge are some of the worst things that ever happened. Their assessment is correct, but it is not the complete picture. There will be no attempt to measure the degree of outrage of any act of discrimination and racism because any one person affected by racism is one person too many.

The sin of Adam and Eve ushered in brokenness in human relationships that not too long after this incident, we have a record of the first murder. Adam and Eve gave birth to two sons, Cain and Abel. Both of them chose two different trades. Cain, who was the older brother, became a farmer and Abel, a shepherd.

These two brothers decided to bring an offering to God. It turns out that things did not go too well for Cain because his offering was not good enough and was rejected by God. This did not sit well with Cain as the following verses report:

And Abel also brought an offering — fat portions from some of the firstborn of his flock. The Lord looked with favor on Abel and his offering, but on Cain and his offering, He did not look with favor. So Cain was very angry, and his face was downcast. Genesis 4:4-5 (NIV)

For the first time, anger is mentioned to describe that state Cain was in. He became angry, apparently driven by jealousy, envy, and hate. Can you imagine how these two brothers have, all of a sudden, become "enemies" because one of them focused intently on what another one was having, instead of on what they were having? Cain might have been driven by fear of his younger brother becoming more than him. According to Cain, God's disapproval of his offering was an indication that his brother Abel was now God's favorite and will be placed above him or get more blessings. It did not cross Cain's mind that he could get a second chance by asking God what he should do so that his own sacrifice would be acceptable in the future.

Cain was not going to work on himself. Instead, he was going to eliminate his brother completely so that there will be no competition. But while he was contemplating this, God tried to reason with him and warned him of the disastrous consequences of not making the right choices. This was an opportunity for Cain to come around and face his own shortcomings, but he was not willing to listen to what God was telling him. God asked him the following questions:

Then the Lord said to Cain, "Why are you angry? Why is your face downcast? If you do what is right, will you not be accepted? But if you do not do what is right, sin is crouching at your door; it desires to have you, but you must rule over it." Genesis 4:6-7 (NIV)

There was still hope for Cain to escape out of his predicament because he was reminded by God that he could rule over sin. The choice was his, and it was within his power to make the right choice. But Cain had made up his mind on what he was going to do: to completely eliminate his own brother, in fact, the only brother he had. This is how Cain went on a devilish act:

> *Now Cain said to his brother Abel, "Let's go out to the field." While they were in the field, Cain attacked his brother Abel and killed him. Genesis 4:8 (NIV)*

Just like the final solution implemented by the Hitler's Nazi Germany that murdered more than six million Jews in the 20th century, we are seeing a firsthand experience of where this idea of eliminating other humans that we are envious of or do not like started. Cain deceived his brother to go out to the field with him, and he attacked him without any warning and brutally murdered him in cold blood.

Why did Cain do such an evil thing against his own flesh and blood? How come these two brothers who looked the same and came from the same household ended up in such a mess? What did Cain think killing his only brother was going to do for him?

I brought up this case of the first murder that was committed by one brother against another to highlight the negative impact the original sin had on the first humans and why we are still having a lot of difficulties getting along with each other today. If two brothers from the same household could not get along with each other, how much more of people from different backgrounds?

We all renounce racism because it causes harm to other people, and in some extreme cases, it has led to murder. This is something that the Encyclopedia of Human Rights states succinctly:

"Racism is completely inconsistent with the core of human rights and antithetical to the realization of all human rights. Racism represents a danger to all human life. It creates intolerance, social divisions, strife, and violence, and can be a social symptom of genocidal tendencies."[1]

---

[1] Quotes & key text excerpts. (2017). In H. V. Conde, *Human rights and the United States* (3rd ed.). Amenia, NY: Grey House Publishing. Retrieved from http://ezproxy. libproxy.db.erau.edu/login?url=https://search.credoreference.com/content/ entry/greyhuman/quotes_andamp_key_text_excerpts/0?institutionId=951

While Cain was not racist towards his brother Abel because there was only one human race, he was motivated by fear, anger, envy, and jealousy. Unfortunately, these vices took the better part of him, and he ended up killing his brother. One can add that Cain stopped looking at his brother Abel as created in the image of God. *There is no way Cain would have attacked his brother if he still valued him.* He allowed his anger and jealousy to cloud his judgment, and he ended up brutally killing his brother because he was no longer human enough in his eyes. The place of his brother had been replaced by the desire to be at the top.

Can you see some of the parallels between what prompted Cain to murder his brother with some of the same things that fuel racism today? People feel that they are better than other people, and the next logical step is to treat those they consider inferior to them in whatever manner they deem appropriate. In the eyes of those perpetuating this havoc, they have the power to do whatever they want. In other words, they have become their own god. We are going to take a closer look at this later on.

The role our senses play in perpetuating racism

In the beginning, after God finished creating the universe and all that is in it was good, God, as we have already seen, gave the five senses so that mankind could enjoy the physical environment and all the good things that God had created. Unfortunately, things did not go as planned because the physical senses were used to break God's law and have since then become the avenue through which the enemy uses to tempt people to disobey God.

We already saw how Eve engaged her five senses to disobey God. This first act of disobedience forever changed the wiring of our five senses because they are now susceptible to be used to do evil. If you trace any evil thing under the sun, it is connected to one of the five senses.

I am focusing on the five senses because racism and discrimination are perpetuated through the five senses as well, especially the sense of hearing, seeing, and touch.

Racism is not a born trait, and there is no such thing as the racist gene. Racism is a learned behavior that is passed down from generation to generation by parents and society. The transmission of racism is facilitated by the five senses because they serve were as a connection between the spiritual and the physical. For example, when a child is born, they have zero racism in them, but over time, the parents and society feed the child with information about other people that looked different. The way this information is shared determines what the child believes about other people. Over time, this information determines how the child interacts with other people and sooner or later, confirmation bias sets in.

This implies that if the child is not taught that other people are inferior or superior, the child will have a different expectation when they meet different people. Unfortunately, this racism virus is being transmitted as parents sit down at the dinner table with their children to eat. At times, the transmission is unconsciously done because of some of the racial jokes and comments that are made. The intention of the parents is not to teach their children racism, but the unintended consequence of such crude jokes is the reinforcement of negative stereotypes about other people. At times, parents are more intentional in teaching their children how to continue perpetuating racism. Take, for example, the parent who gives a stern warning to their child not to get married to a black husband because blacks are not smart enough or prone to a life of crime or whatever reason that may be given to justify why interracial marriages are bad.

Such conversations are not only limited among those who consider themselves superior, those who are being looked down upon to be inferior also have such conversations with their own children. The difference is that they warn their children to stay away from the other people because it will be a betrayal of their own people if they cross the white/black divide. According to them, the whites should not be trusted because they are wicked, selfish, and evil. Most parents think that they are having the best interest of their children at heart and are doing all within their power to protect their children from any harm. But the underlying fear of loss of the position of power and privilege compromises their good intentions and the parents end up passing racism to their children who will, in turn, pass it to their own children.

This has been the case over the years and explains why racism still persists in the world today.

Nobody wants to let their guard down because they are afraid of losing something. It is sad and shocking that some parents still think the worst thing their child can do is get married to somebody of a different race. In some places in Africa, marriages between people from different ethnic groups are frowned upon seriously.

The role of mass media

Even in the age of the internet, which is some sort of an information superhighway, there are a few major actors, such as Google and Facebook, that control the traffic and at times, introduce bias. The mass media houses are using this new information technology to get their messages out as well. In addition to traditional avenues like radio, magazine, and television, the internet is being highly utilized by different mass media organizations.

Mass media is guilty of propagating stereotypes that perpetuate racism because of selective programming and partial reporting. They pick and choose what news items to broadcast and for the sake of ratings, the news focuses on aspects that have a certain appeal to segments of the society, at the expense of other members of the society. Therefore, it will be difficult to talk about the origin and propagation of racism without looking at the role of mass media inseminating information and the impact this information has on race relationships.

Take the case of Africa, which has been described as the dark continent, the white man's grave to a place of extreme poverty, famine, diseases, and death. Nobody is refuting that there is no farming, disease, and death in Africa, but the problem is when the only things that the news outlets in the western world focus on are war, disease, famine, and poverty. Many in the west who have never gone to Africa are having this distorted view that is not true. The fact is that there are famine and suffering in Africa, but many people are also well fed, prosperous, and doing well. Everybody is not living on trees or grass huts, as some in the west want everybody to believe. The question is why so many news outlets only focus on what is wrong with Africa and Africans, but not what is right in Africa? This one-sided, biased reporting has painted a picture of Africa that is false and distorted.

On the flip side, the images and stories that the west feeds into Africa and the rest of the world are carefully staged to give an image of unparalleled prosperity, sophistication, and advancement. The picture of the West that is presented is perfect and flawless that the rest of the world has bought into the lie that in the West, there are no problems. Some even think there is no poverty and no homelessness and no suffering. Technological advances have solved all human problems. This false image of some earthly paradise is far from the reality on the ground in most of these countries.

As you can see, all these positive and negative messages are consumed through our five senses, and they end up forming our opinions about the world around us, including the people that we interact with.

The portrayal of people from different parts of the world is not limited to Africa alone. Most of the so-called third world or less developed or developing countries for lack of a better word are all portrayed in a negative light. Whoever decided that some countries are third world and some are developed and some not-so-developed has contributed to some of the racial tensions across the globe. This is another thing that we will be touching on in later chapters.

Our five senses are the channels through which racism is transmitted. Therefore, any solution to the issue of racism that does not attack it at the level of the senses is hallowed and will not yield any lasting results.

Racism, Tribalism, and Ethnocentrism

It is important to define these important terms before we can dig deeper into their interplay, universality, and how they have all influenced our current understanding of racism because without a proper understanding of what the problem is, we cannot offer adequate solutions. Although racism may mean different things to different people, I will do my best to define it. This definition may not satisfy all parties, but my focus is going to go beyond the definition and focus on how to choke it at the root.

What is racism?

According to the English Oxford Living Dictionaries, racism is defined as

"Prejudice, discrimination, or antagonism directed against someone of a different race based on the belief that one's race is superior."[2]

As you can see, the standard dictionary definition of racism is making the assumption that humans are divided into different races. Because of that, some people may feel that their own race is superior to other races. *It is strange that people have a need to feel superior to others.* According to this definition, racism is based on a "belief that one's race is superior." Where does this belief in superiority come from? What is this belief based on? The short answer is that the belief is baseless and at best, faulty when placed under any serious scrutiny.

It is important to take a different look at how other people define racism. Let us consider the following definition of racism by Conde (2017):

Racism is the mistaken and gratuitous belief that the social construct of race is the primary factor in determining human characteristics and abilities, and that racial differences produce, again mistakenly and gratuitously, inherent superiority of a particular race.[3]

I like the fact that Conde highlights the fallacy in believing that a social contract is valid enough to use it to discriminate against other people. There is one human race and any attempt to divide the human race into different categories, classes or groups is a social construct because there is no such thing as the black race, white race or Asian race. In as much as people like to use this classification, it does not make it true. This is why to fight racism, it is important to start deconstructing some of these social constructs.

What is ethnocentrism?

---

[2] *English Oxford Living, Dictionaries*
[3] Quotes & key text excerpts. (2017). In H. V. Conde, *Human rights and the United States* (3rd ed.). Amenia, NY: Grey House Publishing. Retrieved from http://ezproxy.libproxy.db.erau.edu/login?url=https://search.credoreference.com/content/entry/greyhuman/quotes_andamp_key_text_excerpts/0?institutionId=951

Another word that is of great interest to me because of its propensity to overflow into racism is ethnocentrism. While there is nothing wrong in having a strong affinity for your people who share the same culture, language, beliefs, etc., there is a cause for concern when the "ethnic pride" is turned into prejudice against other ethnicities.

Unfortunately, ethnocentrism is often turned into animosity and bad treatment of other people who do not belong to the dominant or the more affluent group.

The Cambridge English Dictionary defines ethnocentrism as *a belief that a particular race or culture is better than others.*[4]

According to this definition, the feelings of superiority are based on a belief which in many cases is based on nothing more than stereotypes and distorted information about other people and cultures. All cultures are not the same and should not necessarily be because they serve different purposes for those that practice them. But passing value judgment is something that humans are prone to doing, and the conclusions are usually faulty, to say the least.

Here is a more elaborate definition of ethnocentricism by Bagchi, who states that:

"Ethnocentrism is the tendency to place one's own tribe, race, or country at the center of human affairs as superior to other such peoples.[5]

According to Bagchi, *"Ethnocentrism has existed in virtually all societies in human history. To feel superior to other peoples requires that one is aware of others beyond one's national or cultural boundaries. To feel superior to other peoples also requires that one knows enough about others to judge their civilization or way of life as inferior to one's own."*[6]

I have brought up the issue of ethnocentrism here because it is going to be used to bridge the gap between it and tribalism. The concept of tribalism is the brainchild of ethnocentricism driven by western hegemony. When the Europeans came in contact with other

---

[4] Cambridge English Dictionary

[5] Kaushik Bagchi

[6] Berkshire Encyclopedia of World History. Ed. William H. McNeill, Jerry H. Bentley, and David Christian. Vol. 2. Great Barrington, MA: Berkshire Publishing, 2005. p685-688.

civilizations, they decided that these civilizations were backward, primitive and underdeveloped; therefore, these groups should be referred to as tribal. Therefore, the word tribe is loaded with racism, prejudices, and mischaracterization and should be dropped when talking about other people, cultures, and civilizations.

Tribe

It is important to define tribe before tribalism because an attempt will be made to highlight the parallels between these words and how they have influenced and continue to inform our understanding of racism.

The English Oxford Dictionary defines a tribe as *"a social division in a traditional society consisting of families or communities linked by social, economic, religious, or blood ties, with a common culture and dialect, typically having a recognized leader."*[7]

This standard definition uses words like traditional, dialect, and blood ties. Unfortunately, this idea of the tribe which is somehow different from an ethnic group has persisted over time because those who coined the term were trying to distinguish between the more advanced western ethnic groups compared to the primitive, less developed tribal people in other parts of the word.

This is why the Oxford Dictionary had to make this statement in an attempt to sanitize the word tribe and place it in its proper historical context. It says,

"In historical contexts, the word tribe is broadly accepted (the area was inhabited by Slavic tribes), but in contemporary contexts, it is problematic when used to refer to a community living within traditional society. It is strongly associated with past attitudes of white colonialists towards so-called primitive or uncivilized peoples living in remote, undeveloped places. For this reason, it is generally preferable to use alternative terms such as community or people."[8]

In other words, the word tribe was used in the past to justify calling other people primitive and uncivilized. These attitudes of the past have persisted to date because some of these negative stereotypes about

---

[7] *English Oxford Living Dictionaries*
[8] *English Oxford Living Dictionaries*

people from different parts of the world still persist. Many people still look at them using this distorted tribal lens.

The Oxford Dictionary is clearly advocating that the use of the term tribe should be dropped and replaced by "community or people." This is a step in the right direction, but it is not good enough because it has not gone far enough.

I say this has not gone far enough because there is no reason why the word "ethnic" should not be used to refer to subgroups of people, as is the case when referring to subgroups in the west. It is unfortunate that this colonial, biased, tainted name is still popularly being used when talking about people from different parts of the world.

Take, for example, when there was war in the Balkan that led to ethnic cleansing, no single news outlet described what happened in Bosnia, Serbia, and Kosovo as some sort of tribal conflict. None. It was rightfully called an ethnic conflict. But when there was a genocide in Rwanda, people were quick to report about the Tutsi and Hutu tribes cutting each other's throats. The question is, what makes one sub-group of people a tribe and the other an ethnic group? The answer is obvious, but has been ignored and is still being ignored by many. They still continue to call Africans and other so-called uncivilized and primitive people "tribe" for lack of a better term. This is totally unacceptable in this day and age.

While the average person may not care about these subtle relics of stereotypes and bias, it is important to understand the contribution of such classifications on the prevalence of ethnocentrism, discrimination, and racism.

If you take a look at Oxford Dictionary's definition of "ethnic", you will understand the point I am trying to make here. Ethnic is defined as "relating to a population subgroup (within a larger or dominant national or cultural group) with a common national or cultural tradition."[9]

Tribe is *"a social division in a traditional society consisting of families or communities linked by social, economic, religious, or blood ties, with a common culture and dialect, typically having a recognized leader."*[10]

---

[9] *English Oxford Living Dictionaries*
[10] *English Oxford Living Dictionaries*

There is a lot in common between the two. Where you start finding some digression is the idea of blood ties, traditional society, religion, etc., but one can argue that all the so-called ethnic groups have blood ties and share a dominant religion as well. Then why interject tradition in the definition of the tribe to make it become something that it is not?

Traditional does not mean primitive, uncivilized, and backward as many mistakenly think. Traditional, in its purest sense, similarly means that an environment is in its original or natural state and has not been adulterated. How come this has been spun to mean something else? Just because something is in its natural state does not make it primitive and uncivilized.

I have taken a long run to try and explain where I am going because the final objective is to eliminate "tribe" the way it is currently being used to describe the African people and other so-called "primitive and uncivilized people" and replace it with "ethnic" because this is the proper way to look at it.

Now that we have established that the world is made up of different ethnic groups, I am going to circle back to ethnocentrism and look at its propensity to lead to racism.

Tribalism

Before I do that, there is one more term that needs to be defined and contextualized. This is the word tribalism, and it is one of the words that many people use loosely without a second thought. Part of bringing tribalism into this discussion is because as a child, I was taught that my ethnic group and all other ethnic groups in Africa were tribes and still are. Therefore, any conflicts, discrimination, and animosities between the different "tribes" are treated as some sort of tribalism and are somehow on a different category compared to racism.

It seems that because tribal people are considered primitive, savages, underdeveloped and unsophisticated, whatever happens between them is not equal to the sophistication of racism, which is occurring in a more advanced, civilized and sophisticated society. Therefore, let these tribal people do their thing because what else can you expect from uncivilized and primitive people apart from acts of savagery?

While this may not be what is directly communicated by the gatekeepers of civilization, actions speak louder than words and people's attitudes betray them more than they may care to think. This may be why there is so much talk about racism, but the discrimination and animosity between other ethnic groups across the globe are not seen in the same light. It is because this does not fit the narrative or that the damage being done to people in these areas of the world is not painful enough.

All humans bleed when cut. Discrimination, no matter who does it and where it is done, is equally painful, limiting and destructive and should be called out and condemned by all. The time of a two-tier society is gone because tribalism is a bogus term that needs to be eradicated when referring to other people.

So, what is tribalism? The Cambridge English Dictionary has two definitions that caught my attention. The first definition says, *"Tribalism is the state of existing as a tribe or a very strong feeling of loyalty to your tribe."* The second definition is says, *"it is a very strong feeling of loyalty to a political or social group so that you support them whatever they do."*[11]

I have already mentioned that the word tribe is loaded with a lot of negative baggage, especially when used to describe other people, because it was coined by the colonizers to depict those they considered primitive, uncivilized and on the fringes of civilization. These were the tribal people that needed to be colonized and taught how to become civilized. A lot of atrocities were committed against these people and deemed justified just because they were classified as primitive and uncivilized. According to the colonizers, these savages did not know any better and could be treated anyhow.

Therefore, it is important that the first definition of tribalism be discarded and we stick with the second one, which is talking about loyalty to a party of a social group. This makes sense, although some of the excesses of being tribalistic can spill into racism as well.

---

[11] Cambridge English Dictionary

Conclusions on racism, tribalism, and ethnocentrism

I will try to avoid repeating some of what has already been said, but it is important to reiterate the framework within which the issue of racism will be discussed in the rest of the book because we are living in a time when words no longer mean what they originally meant. This is an unfortunate reality, and it makes it difficult to have any meaningful conversation and come up with solutions. Each time you think you have nailed down the problem, the meaning of the words are changed into something else.

For example, the word racism the way it is being used by some in the United States of America right now is synonymous with being a member of the Republican Party. The term has even been expanded to include anybody that voted for President Donald Trump and also those who did not vote for him but have a slight inclination to support any of his policies. Is this the new definition of racism? Or are people invoking this word to keep stoking the flames of hate and animosity among the different people in the country?

While it is understood that the United States of America has had a history filled with a lot of abuse of the African Americans because of hate, prejudices, and all sorts of discrimination and maltreatment, it will be limiting to forget that the country has residents that originally came from every nation under the sun.

Therefore, any attempt to address the issue of racism must incorporate the experiences of all the other nationalities and ethnic groups currently residing in the US because they bring a unique perspective to this issue.

The focus is not on trying to assess the gravity of whatever these people have been through, but on the similarities between these experiences and what drives all of them. We are not going to deny what happened in the past and is still happening, but we should not allow the past to prevent us from paving a new path that will liberate the society from the clutches of racism.

From this point forward, racism is going to be used as a broad term that explains all the unfavorable interactions between all humans. Maybe a new word needs to be coined to describe the feeling of superiority that other people have towards their fellow humans, especially when this feeling is expressed in undesirable ways that cause harm to other people. This can be emotional, physical, economical, and psychological harm.

While one would assume that based on all the research that refutes the division of the human race into different races, this idea that there are different human races is still prevalent may be because of ignorance, for the lack of a better term. This is obviously a common trait among all humans: the desire to take advantage of others and to feel that one is superior to other people. We all hope that more and more people will realize that there is one race: the human race. We also all know that the human race is flawed because of what our first ancestors Adam and Eve did. They disobeyed God, and this unleashed a circle of death and destruction that has been with us since then.

Therefore, trying to understand racial relationships or interactions between different people without factoring in the propensity for any one of us to succumb to treating others in ways that are not kind is refusing the obvious reality that can lead us to better and more permanent solutions.

The limitation of color

Why do we need color to classify humans and divide them into different races? Each time I tell my students that the Mundani language, which I spoke as a child has only three colors, they are shocked. They should be because if you are used to the colors of the rainbow, it will not make sense for you to hear that there are people who see only three colors. I usually ask my students to identify these colors. Most of the students will mention black and white, but the third color always eludes them. I then proceed to let them know that the colors are black, white, and red. Obviously, the next question from the students is "What about yellow, purple, blue, green, etc.?"

I usually tell my students jokingly that we do not care about those colors because we want to keep life simple. Take, for example, green is black in the Mundani language, yellow is red. In other words, all the dark colors are black, and the light colors are red, and white is white.

You may be saying that the Mundani people are not sophisticated enough to identify that there is a difference between yellow and red and yellow should never be called red. There may even be a part of you that is saying that these people are primitive and uncivilized. How could they miss something so obvious as differentiating between green and black? What in the world do they think when they say that green, blue, and purple colors are all black? What about the black color itself? When these people place green, purple and blue side by side, don't they see that the colors are different?

You are right in asking these questions. Unfortunately, there are no answers to these questions because these people live their lives comfortably with just three colors.

Wait a minute! What about those of us who are in more "sophisticated" societies and have fine-tuned the art of color classifications scheme? Are we really that advanced and sophisticated? It seems when it comes to the color of the human skin, we too are "primitive and unsophisticated."

How did we settle down on this white and black classification of the human skin? Or referring to some people as colored? Really? Does this mean that some people are uncolored or what?

By the way, in the Mundani language, white people are called red people maybe because their encounter with whites under tropical conditions revealed that the whites are actually red.

Please bear with me as I point out the absurdity of using color to divide the human race into different races. While society might have accepted this faulty and unfounded color classification scheme, it is time to move away from it. If we want to use color, we should ensure that all the different color skin tones are represented. For example, my hair is black, but my skin is chocolate brown, but I am classified as a black African. I am not trying to refuse or reject the color of my skin, but I am saying that if this must be used, it should properly be identified as such.

The problem with the present sweeping and arbitrary color classification scheme is the baggage that is associated with it. Historically, these colors were used for reasons that were not always good. Consider the case of Africa that was called the dark continent. This was a place of death, crudeness, and backwardness. By implication, her people are dark, and this darkness is associated with evil, monsters, and the devil, to say the least. Dark, impure, backward, primitive, and unsophisticated are not the labels that anybody wants to be associated with. Unfortunately, the so-called black race has been mired with these stereotypes for such a long time that it is almost the norm.

Consider the use of the white color to signify purity, sophistication, advancement, and all that is good. That is why the angels are always clothed in white and the demons in black, even though the Bible says the devil was one of the most beautiful archangels and appears as an angel of light.

Before you dismiss the concerns that have been expressed about the current color classification scheme, you should consider the fact that racism has been fueled and sustained by this color scheme. Whiteness is immediately associated with superiority, sophistication, and advancement. At the same time, black is backward, underdeveloped, and inferior.

If you think this is a bogus claim, you should look at the multi-billion industry of skin lightening cream that is used in all cultures across the globe because it is deeply rooted in some people's psyche that they must lighten their skin to join the "superior class". This is a sad reality that is practiced in every continent, and it is not limited to blacks alone.

Racism, as bogus as it is, will still be used, but it will be used within the confines of the understanding that it is a social construct and has nothing to do with the human race because there is no such thing as the White race, Black race, Asian race, or Hispanic race. For those who insist on saying that there is a Black, White, or whatever race based on the amount of melanin in somebody's skin, I will beg to differ. Nobody ever defines a house solely on its color. Why then should we define human beings based solely on the amount of melanin in their body?

As a geoscientist, it is common knowledge that the color of a mineral is one of the most unreliable characteristics that can be used to describe it. The reason is that some minerals have different colors, for example, you have rose quartz, smoky quartz, milky quartz, amethyst, citrine, etc. The other reason color is not such a good idea is because different minerals have the same color. Therefore, any geologist knows that the best way to test the true color of a mineral is to use the streak of that particular mineral. The streak is the color of the power of the mineral.

Did Martin Luther King, Jr. not say that *"Judge not a man by the color of his skin, but by the content of his character"?* [12]

Dr. King, Jr. was correct, but it seems the society still has to catch up with the reality of what he was talking about. While society may be used to using all these labels to classify people for whatever purpose, these labels have caused more harm than good. There is a lot to a label or a name. It is amazing that each time God wants to do something unique in somebody's life, He changes their name because there is power in what we program in our subconscious minds.

If we as a society say that we are color-blind, then it is time to get rid of the different classes that have been created based on skin color. The war against racism will never be completely won until we start identifying people for who they are, not by whatever color class we place them under. The white/black divide is bogus and has done more harm than good. Some may argue that we are used to these terms and there is no point refusing the fact that there are whites and blacks. It seems when it comes to white, we just created a new color because I have yet to see somebody that looks like a white sheet of paper. In other words, the white we call white is actually a social construct that is false. Therefore, this supports that idea that the use of color to classify humans does not have the right intentions. It is a tool of discrimination, subjugation, and control.

Now is the time to move beyond using color to identify people. We are all humans and should be looked upon as that. It is absurd to use the color of somebody's skin to classify them or worse, force them into some arbitrary human race. You can help by stop calling people black or white. Call them by their name, and this is good enough.

While some take pride in the so-called blackness or whiteness, it is a false identity that should be discarded by all. We are humans, and each and every one of us has a name that should be used to identify us. If we want to put an end to racism, society must make a conscious decision to move away from this skin color classification that is currently being used.

---

[12] https://www.cbsnews.com/news/mlks-content-of-character-quote-inspires-debate/

I am acutely aware of the fact that dropping off the current classification scheme will not resolve the issue of racism because the problem, as we are going to see, is deeper than skin color and bigger than racism itself. All society is doing is using racism to dress a far dangerous problem that has plagued mankind since the Garden of Eden.

We are going to realize that to find our way out of this quagmire, we must go back to where things went terribly wrong. It is time to go back to the Garden of Eden and see if there are clues to the way forward for humanity. It has been said that the definition of insanity is doing the same thing but expecting to achieve different results. What we are used to is calling people racist, hateful and bigoted. This has not achieved anything because racism is still here. Many laws have been passed to curb racism, and this has brought some limited success because laws may constrain people and deter them from manifesting the intent of their hearts, but they do not change hearts. This is why segregation is still rampant at 9:00 am on Sunday mornings across the United States of America.

Before you get excited that I am touching the root of the problem, I would like to remind you that the segregation that we see each Sunday morning is not just between whites and blacks. It is also between blacks and blacks. For example, people from Nigeria still get segregated according to different Nigerian ethnic groups. One of the reasons is that people like "their own", the familiar, predictable, and comfortable. However, we are not supposed to only focus on what is comfortably familiar and predictable because, in the long run, it erodes social cohesion. To know each other and dismantle some of the prevalent stereotypes, there is a need for all people to interact with each other under different circumstances.

Chapter 2:
The Complex Interplay of Superiority and Inferiority

There are two kinds of pride, both good and bad. 'Good pride' represents our dignity and self-respect. 'Bad pride' is the deadly sin of superiority that reeks of conceit and arrogance. John C. Maxwell

As I already stated, racism is not just a white and black issue because in every society on the face of the earth, there are two major groups of people: those who feel they are superior and those who have been forcefully made to feel that they are inferior. This superiority is driven by fear and greed. There is never any justification for taking advantage of other people, but for this to happen, people have to be reduced to something less than they actually are. *When people have been bombarded with a lie for a long time, they believe it.* People will keep living this lie because their subconscious minds have been programmed by this faulty information. The subconscious mind cannot distinguish between what is true and what is false. The subconscious mind believes whatever information is fed into it and will use that information to determine the action each particular individual takes.

While racism has been amplified in societies like the United States of America where the arbitrary white/black divide has heightened this issue, we should not be distracted by the "intensity" of this problem. Unfortunately, many have cast racism as something that exists strictly between the white and black races. This way of looking at the issue has not helped us solve the problem, and it is the highest time that we try a new approach.

In the previous chapter, I tried to debunk the notion of different human races and established that we are all created in the image of God, and therefore, there is only one human race. *In addition to the fact that there is only one human race, using color to classify humans is absurd and baseless.* The society may insist on using this arbitrary classification scheme, but it is faulty and must be discarded.

If there is only one human race, then the term racism itself needs to be redefined or discarded altogether.

Conde (2017) defines racism as *"the mistaken and gratuitous belief that the social construct of race is the primary factor in determining human characteristics and abilities, and that racial differences produce, again mistakenly and gratuitously, inherent superiority of a particular race."*[13]

As this definition clearly states racism is a social construct, then the belief in superiority is faulty as well. This social construct is arbitrary and should be discarded because grouping humans in different races are based on skin color, which as we have already seen, is faulty.

The definition highlights the issue of superiority that is at the heart of ethnocentrism, and it is common among all the ethnic groups on every continent on the planet. When ethnocentrism is not checked, it spills into discrimination, mistreatment and, at times, death.

Therefore, instead of isolating and treating the manifestation of "ethnocentrism gone amok" that exists between the white and black races, we should be looking at interactions within the entire human race because this broad division between white and black is artificial and unfounded.

Removing the white and black divide does not eliminate the discrimination, hate, and murder that occurs between different humans, regardless of their geographic location. I started by looking at the first murder that occurred between two brothers from the same parents.

---

[13] Quotes & key text excerpts. (2017). In H. V. Conde, *Human rights and the United States* (3rd ed.). Amenia, NY: Grey House Publishing. Retrieved from http://ezproxy. libproxy.db.erau.edu/login?url=https://search.credoreference.com/content/entry/greyhuman/quotes_andamp_key_text_excerpts/0?institutionId=951

You would have expected these two brothers to live in harmony, but something went wrong, and one of the brothers killed the other.

Remember that these two brothers had never heard the word racism and had no socio-economic division or any class distinction whatsoever. This did not prevent anger, fear, envy, and jealousy from driving one of them to murder the other. Therefore, it will be naïve to invoke racism to be the root cause of what happened here. It seems there is something deeper at play here. When we dig a little deeper, we find out that the parents of these two brothers were living in a state of perfection until their disobedience brought in Sin, death, and destruction.

From that point to date, the human race has had a difficult time relating and living in harmony with each other because humankind is out of harmony with the Creator. Although we are can easily get distracted by the so-called manifestation of racism, the issue is deeper than that. I have already established that race is a social construct, and it is not real. It is some sort of a camouflage that is used to cover up a deeper and more serious problem.

Nobody can say that "Racism caused me to discriminate against some other person, treat them badly, segregate them, enslave, lynch, and murder them with impunity." Therefore, we must dig deeper and look for the root cause of all the hate, resentment, and wickedness that people express towards one another. How can anybody in their right minds pin slavery on the skin color? The "blacks" were not enslaved because of their skin color. We must also factor in that other "blacks" in Africa caught and sold their brethren to the Europeans and Arabs. Yes, the Arabs were buying and selling Africans long before the Europeans jumped onto this profitable business that was fueled by greed and despicable evil. Words are not adequate to describe this dark page in human history. While we may be tempted to place it above all other terrible events, we should not forget that human history is punctuated by such despicable acts that humans carried out against each other.

Therefore, we should resist the temptation of reducing such depths of depravity with racism because racism pales in comparison to what is hidden deep within the heart of man. All our attempts over the years to address the symptoms of this problem have not taken us far because abolishing racism will never be possible if the root cause is not attacked.

A few thousand years ago, the prophet Jeremiah, under the inspiration of the Holy Spirit, wrote the following chilling words:

"The heart is deceitful above all things,

And desperately wicked;

Who can know it? Jeremiah 17:9 New King James Version (NKJV)

Let us go back to the two brothers and take a close look at Cain's heart. God saw anger, bitterness, and resentment in his heart and warned him that if he did not do something, he was going to yield to sin. Cain decided to hide the wickedness in his heart from his brother. That is why when he invited his brother to come to the field with him, the unsuspecting brother showed up. If Abel could read his brother's heart, he would have found out that his brother was planning to murder him. This would have prevented him from going.

Nobody can read the wickedness that is in people's hearts. When Abel showed up, his brother Cain suddenly attacked and murdered him.

People may try to justify their mistreatment of other people under racism, but I am saying that racism is a toothless bulldog. It is a bogeyman that is being used to mask the wickedness in the hearts of mankind. There is no way a baseless, absurd, and unfounded social construct has the power to force people to commit heinous crimes against other people. It is time to stop blaming racism and start accepting that people are capable of doing terrible things to each other.

An issue of the heart

Whatever causes people to hate, discriminate, and at times, murder others is an issue of the heart. We have already mentioned that the heart of man is desperately wicked. Out of a wicked heart flows all sorts of evil things, that the heart is where we need to focus our efforts when trying to address the issue of racism. A desperately wicked human heart needs deliverance. There is no way the amount of melanin in somebody's skin will justify enslaving, mistreating, or taking advantage of them.

You may be saying that racism is real because of the historical records of the enslavement for people from Africa, and the lynchings in the southern parts of the US, segregation, Jim Crow and the civil rights movement, etc. This is just part of the picture and a manifestation of a deeper problem. The Africans that ended up in chains in the US and whose descendants were subjected to all sorts of inhumane treatment were originally caught and sold by fellow Africans. This point is being raised here not to blame or castigate anybody, but to point out the depravity in every human heart and to underscore the fact that given the right circumstances, ALL humans, no matter their skin color, are capable of committing terrible acts against other humans.

Therefore, instead of focusing on racism, which is just a symptom of a sick, desperately wicked human heart, we should be looking at the heart. Take, for example, the terrible events that led to the Holocaust of six million Jews. Did this barbaric act have anything to do with skin color or was it driven by the evil in the hearts of the perpetrators who raised other bogeymen in the name of the master race to justify slaughtering millions of people?

We must peel back this camouflage and get to the evil in the hearts of people that is manifested in acts of violence, hate, discrimination, etc.

If you doubt the havoc that the heart of man can cause, it is important to consider what Jesus Christ said concerning the heart. Some of the teachers of the law were accusing the disciples of Jesus Christ for eating without following some of the ceremonial laws of washing of hands. Jesus, in their defense, said, After Jesus said this, the people were not satisfied with His response. He had to explain further:

What goes into someone's mouth does not defile them, but what comes out of their mouth, that is what defiles them." Matthew 15: 11 (NIV)

"Are you still so dull?" Jesus asked them. "Don't you see that whatever enters the mouth goes into the stomach and then out of the body? But the things that come out of a person's mouth come from the heart, and these defile them. **For out of the heart come evil thoughts—murder, adultery, sexual immorality, theft, false testimony, slander.** *These are what defile a person; but eating with unwashed hands does not defile them." Matthew 15: 16-20 (NIV)*

We are back to where we started. These things that come out of the heart are bad and nobody wants or likes them. For example, when a police officer guns down an unarmed black male, there is outrage and outcries of racism. The reasoning is that the likes of Michael Brown were shot because of their skin color, but the reason may be deeper than the fact that the police officer is white and the victim black. According to Jesus Christ, there is something more sinister at work here, and it is the state of the heart. Everything that happens on the outside is a result of what is happening on the inside.

In order words, if a person is not having hate, murder, evil thoughts, there is no way they will allow the color of somebody's skin to prompt them to shoot indiscriminately. While some may argue that it is the chicken-and-the-egg situation, in this situation, I will argue that external factors reveal the true intent of the heart. If the heart is not wicked and already evil, it will not become evil overnight.

People are not naturally good

Here, I refer to all people on the planet, regardless of where they are, who they are, and their socio-economic status. *You may be shocked to hear that no one is good.* We may pretend that we are good because the wickedness in our hearts has not been made manifest, but under the right circumstances, our true nature will come out and most of the time, it is not something that we are proud of. Just because you do things and you get away without being caught does not mean that we are any better than those who were caught and punished.

You may be protesting that you are good and know good people. I am not going to argue with you because if you are using external judgments to say people are good, then you are right. But nobody can decipher what is in another person's heart. This is where you will be seriously mistaken to think that you are good and other people are. It is even possible to do good deeds, but those good deeds do not automatically qualify you to be a good person. Jesus gave a laundry list of the things that are found in the heart that make us not good.

If you are still insisting that you are good and know some very good people, I want you to take a close look at this exchange between Jesus Christ and a young rich ruler:

As Jesus started on His way, a man ran up to him and fell to his knees before Him. "Good teacher," he asked, "what must I do to inherit eternal life?"

"Why do you call me good?" Jesus answered. **"No one is good—except God alone.** *You know the commandments: 'You shall not murder, you shall not commit adultery, you shall not steal, you shall not give false testimony, you shall not defraud, honor your father and mother."*

"Teacher," he declared, "all these I have kept since I was a boy."

Jesus looked at him and loved him. "One thing you lack," he said. "Go, sell everything you have and give to the poor, and you will have treasure in heaven. Then come, follow me."

At this, the man's face fell. He went away sad, because he had great wealth.

Jesus looked around and said to His disciples, "How hard it is for the rich to enter the kingdom of God!" Mark 10: 17-23 (NIV)

Here is somebody who had kept all the laws and would have passed for a good man, yet when he met Jesus, it turned out that he still had some serious issues that he needed to deal with. Jesus stated categorically that only God is good. Unless you are God, you cannot claim to be good.

God's standard of being good is extremely high, but the purpose is not to condemn us but to point us to His goodness that is available to all of us through His son Jesus Christ.

To show you how high and impossible God's standard is, I want you to consider the following Jesus said regarding murder and adultery:

"You have heard that it was said to the people long ago, 'You shall not murder, and anyone who murders will be subject to judgment.' But I tell you that anyone angry with a brother or sister will be subject to judgment. Again, anyone who says to a brother or sister, 'Raca,' is answerable to the court. And anyone who says, 'You fool!' will be in danger of the fire of hell." Matthew 5:21-22 (NIV)

Jesus said if you are angry with your brother or sister, you are going to be brought to judgment, just like somebody who murdered a brother or a sister. Do you remember that before Cain murdered his brother

Abel, he was angry? How many good people you know who are also angry people? What about you? Are you an angry person?

> *"You have heard that it was said, 'You shall not commit adultery.' But I tell you that anyone who looks at a woman lustfully has already committed adultery with her in his heart." Matthew 5:27-28 (NIV)*

If you are still arguing that people are naturally good and you can tell by observing them externally, here is another verse that challenges that idea. Adultery is not only when you actually do it, but when you lust in your heart based on what you see or think. Can you also predict or decipher if somebody is lusting in their heart?

Lastly, you should consider the following verse that is talking about the state of all mankind. The verse clearly states:

> *For all have sinned and fall short of the glory of God. Romans 3:23-27 (NKJV)*

All here includes you and me. Sin simply means missing the mark. Adam and Eve were the first people to miss the mark when they disobeyed God and chose to listen to the lies of the devil. Through them, all of us became sinners because we are directly descended from them. As it is written in the following verse, anybody born on this earth had been "contaminated" by Adam and Eve's sin.

> *For as by one man's disobedience many were made sinners, so also by one Man's obedience, many will be made righteous. Romans 5:19 (NKJV)*

We are Adam's descendants and have been "contaminated" by his sin. Therefore, we are not inherently good and are capable of producing good works that meet God's standard. The good news is that through the obedience of Jesus Christ, He has paved the way for everybody who wills to receive God's righteousness. This implies that we can actually become good after the life of God gets into us. It is only after we have been reconciled and reconnected to God that we can start producing good works that meet God's standard of what is truly good.

Facts do not lie, and the truth will always prevail. Some people have completely rejected the notion of sin and God's righteous standard, and that humans, through their own efforts alone, can become good. Well, you need to turn on the news, go to prison, and see for yourself firsthand evidence of the havoc that sin is causing on our society.

Refusing that sin does not exist and wishing it to go away has not helped at all. People, by default, are not good, and out of them are deeds that are harmful to other people. The manifestation of racism is a direct result of sin. In other words, racism is a symptom of sin that plagues all mankind.

You may be wondering why I am introducing the issue of sin and emphasizing that nobody is good except God. The reason is that as much as we want to restrict racism to something that is predominant between blacks and whites, we cannot because racism is universal and every human is capable of discriminating against other people. This assertion is not trivializing the seriousness of this problem, but it is highlighting how serious and universal this problem actually is.

There is no society on earth that you will not find the manifestation of these issues of the heart: "evil thoughts — murder, adultery, sexual immorality, theft, false testimony, slander, fear, greed, hate, etc." We are aware that when we say somebody is a racist, it is because the person has manifested one or more of these issues of the heart. These issues of the heart have a serious negative impact on other people when expressed by those we consider racist. If racism had no adverse effect on people, it would not be a problem at all, but we know that racism has the potential of destroying lives, and at times, it literally does that.

We have clearly seen that racism is just a smoke screen. It is masking a more serious problem, which is the sin in the hearts of people. To resolve the problem of racism, sin has to be identified and dealt with. If we continue to ignore sin and try to legislate away the problem, we will continue to get limited success because we are just adding Band-Aid to a decaying and stinking wound. Now is the time to make some changes and get to the root of the problem of racism. There is no point in focusing on the symptoms because it is not delivering the outcome that we desire and need.

Hurting people hurt others

The human race is hurting because of the disobedience of Adam and Eve. The original harmony that was disrupted in the beginning has been replaced by death, sickness, and decay.

We all know that racism is bad because of the negative impact it has on other people. But the question is, why do people hate, discriminate, and treat other people wrong? Why does somebody need to feel that they are superior to others? In short, why can't all of us just get along? How can another human being think that others are subhuman because of where and who gave birth to them?

You can be in a country where the caste system is prevalent, and they may justify it one way or the other, but there is no justification to relegating people to a position of servitude for life. Any system that imposes limitations on who goes where, who interacts with who, and gets married to who needs to be re-examined.

Those who need to feel superior over other people are suffering from a superiority complex and need to get down from their high horse. Just because somebody or a group of people think they are superior does not necessarily mean that they are superior.

Even if they feel that they are superior, it does not make it true. People deal with their hurt in different ways, and some think that feeling superior over other humans give them a sense of power and purpose. Nothing can fill the void that is in the heart of each one of us. This is the void that only God can fill, but throughout human history, people have tried everything under the sun to fill this void to no avail.

If you meet somebody who thinks that another human being is beneath their feet and they are ready to discredit them because of the amount of melanin in their skin, you should pity that person because they are hurting badly and need healing. There is no iota of data that supports some of the absurd ideas about the human race that is perpetuated across the globe.

When you take a close look at how people interact with each other, you will realize that ignorance and misinformation are driving most of the beliefs and attitudes people have towards each other.

Every country in the world has hurting people. The entire world is filled with hurting people, and these hurting people are hurting other people. To reduce this monstrous human problem to racism is trivializing this issue. Ever since people started blaming racism as the cause of the hate, anger, mistreatment, and even murder of other people, the issue of racism has not been resolved. Instead, racism is on the rise and the definition as has morphed into something entirely different, depending on where you are.

Lately, there have been talks of racism on the rise in Europe because of the influx of immigrants from other parts of the world. Again, the news media like sensational headlines and focuses on the symptoms, rather than the root cause. The symptoms make good viewing, but does not necessarily try to resolve the problem.

Fear is a stronger emotion than racism, and fear is usually driven by ignorance. The word "ignorance" here is used not as an insulting term, but to explain a lack of information. When you have an influx of people into an area with customs, beliefs and other ways of doing things that are very different from those of the people in their new environment, there is bound to be some distress on both parties.

On the one hand, those that feel their space is being invaded will try to push back because they are afraid that their way of life is being threatened. In addition to the fear of losing their way of life, there is a fear of limited resources, jobs, and depressing wages. The other big fear is an increase in crime.

These fears are not limited in Europe or North America alone. These reactions are common among people all over the world. Each time people move into an area, other people may feel threatened and become fearful.

I remember hearing some derogatory terms being used to describe people from the northwest region of Cameroon that has moved into the soutwestern region of the country. Some of the southwesterners started feeling that these "strangers" are taking their lands, their women, and most of the economic opportunities. This led to some tension, and at one point, some were calling the Northwesterners "come to no go." This was a reminder to those of northwest region descent that they do not belong here and will never be considered part of this part of the country. According to this reason, once you move in from somewhere else, you will always be treated as an outsider. Can you imagine this type of sentiment among people that have the same skin color, share a lot, and are citizens of the same country?

Hurting people indeed hurt others, and this is a universal problem and should not be reduced to a white and black problem. While there are different degrees of the manifestation of this problem, the underlying characteristics of hate, discrimination, mistreatment, and murder have cut across every society, culture, and nation.

As I write this, Cameroon, my country of birth, has had an armed rebellion for the past two years that has led to the displacement of hundreds of thousands of people. My parents have fled their home as well and are living somewhere else. Thousands of others are living in the bushes. Many lives have been lost, and many are still going to be lost because, with each passing day, that situation is getting direr.

Cameroon has a complicated history. After the Berlin conference of 1884, Africa was portioned and the Germans were given the territory called Kamerun. They colonized and administered this territory until the first world war broke out. The British and French troops invaded Kamerun from the West and East, respectively and were able to flush out the Germans. The Western part of Kamerun that was occupied by the British was carved out as a British territory and named Southern Cameroons, while the Eastern part occupied by the French was called East Cameroun.

In 1960, French Cameroun gained her independence from France and became the Republic of Cameroun. In 1961, a plebiscite was conducted by the United Nations in Southern Cameroons to determine their future. They had to vote to join Nigeria or the La Republic du Cameroun. When all the ballots were counted, those in favor of joining La Republic du Cameroun won.

The two countries decided to form the Federal Republic of Cameroon. In 1972, there was another vote and the country became the United Republic of Cameroon, technically getting rid of the federal system of government that had issued each part of the country to conduct their affairs in a manner that gave them dignity, respect, and honor. Those from the English side of the country, since they were in the minority, started feeling that those from the French side were trying to absorb them and erase their identity. Some accused those from the French side of forcing the United Republic without honoring the terms under which the two countries came together in the first place.

In 1984, the president got up and declared that the country was now La Republic du Cameroun. This effectively erased the history of the union between two countries and set the stage for the Recolonization of the Anglophone part of the country. The French side is in the majority and has been slowing choking the English side. About two years ago, those in the English side felt that the oppression, marginalization, mass incarcerations, indiscriminate killings, discrimination, and lack of opportunities were unbearable. After peaceful demonstrations and protest did not yield the desired results, some of the people have taken up arms. Now, the separatist groups are seeking to create their own country where they will be free, respected, treated with dignity, and have equal opportunities for all. They will no longer be judged by the language they speak and will not be discriminated against because they cannot speak the French language, and will have fair trials because the common law, not the French legal system, is used to try them.

What is happening in Cameroon is not restricted to Cameroon. There are people all over the world that feel they are in the minority and are being discriminated against, have no opportunities, treated unfairly, murdered, abused, hated, and all sorts of atrocities. No matter what justification is given to explain why those in the majority were doing this to minorities when you dig deep, you will find that even those in the majority are hurting. Being in the majority does not spare you from the malady of the heart (envy, greed, hate, murder, slander, wickedness, adultery, lust, fornication, bribery, etc.).

The key point of the matter is that hurting people hurt people, and there are hurting people in every country in the world, regardless of nationality, level of education, political, religious affiliation, and social status.

Therefore, it is more appropriate to focus on what is causing people to be hurt, not on racism, which is just a result of the hurt. If we can solve this hurt in the hearts of people, the problem of racism and other issues will be resolved.

The driver of superiority complex

It is important for us to understand that the phenomena of superiority and inferiority complexes have existed in all human societies through the ages. Today, no matter where you go, you will find that the society is broadly divided into two main groups: those that think they are superior to others and those who have been relegated, forced or brainwashed to believe that they are inferior. We may be splitting hairs to get to the intricacies of these phenomena, but each society has different ways of classifying who is superior and who is inferior. In some cases, the amount of money and material possessions you have define your position. In other countries, the social class or caste in which somebody is born determines if they are considered inferior or superior. Whatever arbitrary criteria are used to divide people into these two broad categories is not based on any facts that can be substantiated.

All humans are equal because when all the external and material trappings are stripped, the human spirit is the same. Our true essence is our spirit, and it is a distraction when we focus solely on the body. This is why using skin color to determine somebody's worth is so inhumane, degrading, insulting, and demeaning. It is also why many people are completely opposed to any form of racism, and rightfully so, because it takes away human dignity and reduces people to something they were not created to be. All were created with and endowed with equal rights that should not be usurped by anybody, government, or political ideology.

Now, let us take a look at the history and some of the drivers of superiority and inferiority complexes. We will start with a broad look at the interaction of Europeans with other people, not because the Europeans are the worst offenders. When you look throughout human history, from Egypt, the cradle of civilization, through the Babylonians, Persians, Roman, Byzantine, Mayan, Aztecs and modern history, you will see some similarities between the conquered and their conquerors. We are not trying to classify who did the most evil here or committed the most egregious crimes against humanity. The purpose of highlighting this interplay of superiority and inferiority complexes is to show that it is a common human problem that has occurred throughout all human history and is still alive and well today. Therefore, we should be careful not to pin it on a single group of people. The temptation to do so is extremely strong because what the Europeans did during the last few centuries of human history is still fresh in our minds. We are living with some of the realities today, and it is going to take a while to resolve some these issues.

Take the case of Africa. In 1884, Europeans gathered in Berlin and only portioned the continent between themselves, each European power grabbing whatever chunk of Africa they considered juicy enough for their attention. They cared little about the impact these arbitrary lines were going to have on the continent. They also did not have any regard for all the different independent countries that were already existing within these carved-out territories. Some of their arbitrary lines divided different ethnic groups and placed them under different countries where different languages were imposed on them. In some cases, a part of the same Kingdom was placed under French rule and the other under English rule.

When these territories were colonized and arbitrarily declared nations, they had the mistaken assumption that separate independent kingdoms made of up different ethnicities will just get along. You do not impose a nation on people who are not ready or willing to be part of a nation. The colonizers had a nonchalant attitude towards these "primitive natives": all they had to do was toe the line and do what their "masters" demanded. After all, the Europeans knew better than the Africans and could impose on them whatever they deemed necessary. To effectively administer these artificially created countries, the colonizers used intimidation, propaganda, subjugation, and distortion of information to strip the colonized of their sense of dignity, self-worth, and purpose.

It is worth noting that colonization was not an act of charity because it was driven by some of the issues of the heart I have already mentioned. At this particular point in history, most of the European powers colonized other countries driven partly by the industrial revolution that started in Britain. They needed raw materials for their industries and they need markets to sell their finished goods. These European powers were not only interested in trading with these countries, but they want to subjugate, occupy, and rule over them.

We are talking about independent countries that were taking good care of their affairs without any outside intervention. My ethnic group, which I will call the Bamumbu people, was an independent kingdom ruled by my great-great-grandparents. The kingdom of Bamumbu was independent and free from any outside interference. It had warriors that defended the kingdom from any outside influences. Our encounter with the Europeans destroyed the kingdom, and what is left now is nothing compared to what it was. We still have a king, but his powers have been curtailed, and his influence has been reduced tremendously.

You may be wondering how the Europeans succeeded in subduing other countries. Each country used different tactics. The English specialized in indirect rule, while the French mastered direct rule. The common thread is that the Europeans figured out a way to present themselves as superior to the other people that they met. This behavior, as I already stated, is not unique to the Europeans. The Romans are guilty of it; the Arabs and all the major powers that conquered and ruled over other people did it, too.

The process of subjugating other people starts with devaluing them and creating a false image about them, to the point that they believe it and start perpetuating it. The people had to be distracted from what they had for it to be taken away from them or bought at extremely poor prices. For example, when you visit many European countries, you see much artwork and artifacts that were looted from all over the world. The natives were made to understand that their art was primitive, demonic, and should be discarded. These people happily gave them away, among many other things, to embrace this new, superior, and more sophisticated way of doing things. The Spaniards looted and pillaged South America as well. The Indian subcontinent was not spared from British dominance and exploitation for over 300 years.

Before the British occupied India and the large French areas of Africa, we know that the Arabs had had their own share of occupying other lands, making the people of these lands their subjects, and exploiting them. Many people know about the transatlantic slave trade, but very little is said about the trans-Sahara slave trade that was perpetuated by the Arabs. The Africans that were taken across the Sahara desert to the Middle East ended up working under deplorable conditions. Some of them were castrated to become eunuchs that serve their kings.

I am opening a can of cankerworms here, and rightfully so, because it is important for us to understand the source of the lingering sense of superiority and inferiority complexes that exist in the world right now. I am not in any way trying to get into the blame game here because that is a dead end and no good will come out of it. Africa, India, South America, and all the other countries that were occupied in recent history are not the first to experience conquest. Human history is filled with examples of conquest, occupation, enslavement, and dominance of one group of people over the other. Any attempt to try and use today's understanding to judge the past without placing everything within the context of past circumstances is doing a disservice and will be causing more harm than good.

We are looking at the past so that we can understand the lingering feeling of superiority that some have, while others feel that they are inferior because of the disinformation that has been fed to them for a long time. Again, this visit to the past is not intended for analysis paralysis and to play the blame game. We have already established that no one is good, and all have the propensity to take advantage of others if the conditions are ripe. This is not an attempt to minimize or downplay the ills of the past because it affected real people and we are still leaving with some of the consequences today. That said, this book is about hope and the way forward. If we keep looking at what is behind us, we will miss what is before us and we will never get out of the present sense of hurt and hopelessness.

We look at the past so that we can have a better grasp of what is happening right now. Some of the legacies of the past superiority complex are still being manifested today. For example, somebody in the United States of America asked me if we have houses in Cameroon. I could not help but wonder if they thought I was living on some tree. What about the US embassy in Cameroon? Is the embassy on some tree as well? I had just moved to the United States as an international student, and somebody asked me this question, and it was more than a shock. If somebody thinks that people from Africa are living on trees, then they have a lot of learning to do. Instead of taking offense, I pitied this particular individual for being misinformed and for believing a lie.

Not too long ago, we were having dinner in our home when our guest popped the following question: "I have heard that there are monkeys, chimpanzees, and other wildlife that roam the streets in Africa. Is this true?" I took it as an opportunity to educate my guest about Africa. I called one of our daughters to bring my iPad and I was able to pull up a few pictures of the capital of Cameroon to show this person that instead of monkeys and chimpanzees, the streets are occupied by people and vehicles. My guest was surprised that the city looked like any "modern city." I could have become offended, but I chose to educate. We are living in the information age, and most of the stereotypes about other people can easily be debunked by already existing information. All people need to do is to search for that information.

Unfortunately, many have been fed with such faulty information since when they were kids that it is proving almost impossible to help these people see things differently.

Some people think that they are better than others and even take the liberty to act on these thoughts and discriminate against other people. Those who think they are better than others are living in self-delusion. There is one race, the human race, and we are all equal, although not the same. It is unfortunate that physical features such as the pigmentation of one's skin, the color of their hair and shape of their nose is used to define who they are. Who in their right mind will say that the color of a house defines the house? This type of thinking is not based on any facts, but people are delusional, thinking they have their facts straight.

Racism is driven by fear, ignorance, greed, and selfishness. There is no scientific evidence for the subdivision of the human race, so all these divisions are social constructs that have no empirical basis.

However, the notion of the black race, white race, and many other subdivisions persist because of ignorance and fear. It appears some like the present status quo because 1) it serves them better, and 2) it places other people at a disadvantageous position. I am aware that this type of reasoning will take us to a dead end because those perpetuating race divisions for one reason other the others are fighting hard to ensure that things do not change because they fear they will lose something. Some of the people who feel that race divisions have hurt and placed them at a disadvantageous position want to hold on the hurt because it brings them sympathy. Meanwhile, those who have benefited from race divisions want to keep these benefits.

There is a better way, though. First, it is important to understand that the final say rests with each individual. Just because somebody thinks, believes, and even acts as if he or she is superior to others does not mean this is true. What parameters is this individual using to access their superiority? Those who dare believe that they are superior to others and act accordingly are to be pitied because they are not well-informed.

It is sad that many people are allowing the ignorance of other people to influence how they view themselves and what they believe about themselves. Let God be true and let any other person be wrong. It is written that you are fearfully and wonderfully made, and that you are the apple of God's eye and was created in His image and likeness. If you believe this, then racism will bow at your feet. You do not have any other option than to believe what your Creator says about you. When you buy a car or any other appliance, it comes with the manufacturer's manual. If the manufacturer, for example, says that your car needs gasoline, you dare not put diesel in the engine because you will ruin it. You faithfully follow the manufacturer's recommendations because you trust the manufacturer. Anybody in their right mind will follow what the manufacturer says.

You have been created by God, and the Bible, which is God's word, is the handbook that contains the instructions on what to feed your mind with. It also has information on what you are made out of and what the designer had in mind when you were created. Therefore, you must and should listen to manufacturer and not other end-users. Whatever the society says or thinks cannot override what God has said about you. You are wonderfully and fearfully made.

What you believe about yourself is what people sense when they meet you. As such, you must feed your mind with the right information about you. It does not matter what the government says or what the society says because you are not what other people define you to be, even if it is written in textbooks and broadcasted over TV and the radio. People's opinion about you should never be allowed to become your reality. You must refuse it and replace it with what your Creator says about you. Period.

Therefore, instead of trying to change the racist, focus on changing your belief system. For racism to work, it needs two kinds of people: those who, out of ignorance, believe and act as if they are superior and those who believe that they are inferior because they have been told they are. You may be saying right now that racism goes beyond what happens between two individuals, that it is institutionalized and sanctioned by the laws in some countries. Any man-made laws that place limitations on other people based on race and bias, the social construct must be challenged and called out for what they truly are. This is where laws must be passed to counteract institutionalized racism. In some countries, good laws have been passed to fight racism and discrimination, but the laws alone will not deliver. As good as laws may sound on paper, they cannot change the issues of the heart. In the meantime, you must continue to work on yourself, and when you become valuable enough, you will be sought after.

By the way, waiting for other people to accept you before you accept yourself is relinquishing the power of having the final say into the hands of others. It is a terrible idea to wait for the approval of others before you become comfortable in your own skin. You must lead the way by finding yourself and being happy for who you are and not wait for others to give you their approval to be who you are. Resist the pressure from society and social media to want to define who you are — they will never get it.

Chapter 3:
Telling It Like It Is

Racism comes in many different forms. Sometimes it's subtle, and sometimes it's overt. Sometimes it's violent, and sometimes it's harmless, but it's definitely here. It's something that I think we're all guilty of, and we just have to make sure that we deal with our own personal racism in the right way. Jordan Peele

The assumption in society today, especially in societies where the black race and white races interact, is that racism is prevalent. When people operate under this social construct, they are bound to assume that the manifestation of the issues of the heart (such as greed, selfishness, fear, envy, jealousy, and wickedness) is a result of racism. In the previous chapter, the whole idea of race was debunked because there is only one race: the human race. Any other divisions are baseless and mere social constructs. The idea of racism itself is based on a faulty understanding of the human race and the false assumption that some people are inferior. These assumptions are wrong because nobody is superior to another, and it is wrong to use the color of somebody's skin to define who they are. I demonstrated that color is very unreliable and should never be used to classify people.

When we throw color out and throw racism out, ethnocentricism moves in to fill the void. Ethnocentricism becomes bad when the desire to support your own people conditions you to exclude, exploit, discriminate, maltreat and, in some cases, hate and murder other people that do not look like you, eat, dress, believe and speak like your own group.

You will realize that since the original harmony between God and our ancestors Adam and Eve was broken, the relationship between people is broken as well. This brokenness is manifested through the excesses of ethnocentricism that, in many cases, has been given a pass, and racism used as a scapegoat.

I am going to expose the hypocrisy of many who scream at the racism between whites and blacks. These people behave similarly, discriminating against other people because they do not look like them in one way or the other. This behavior is driven by fear and ignorance.

I was told not to marry a foreign woman

You will have to read this portion carefully and between the lines to understand what I am trying to say. Make sure that you do not draw any rash conclusions and misunderstand what I am about to say. I do not like the blame game because it gives to much power to other people and circumstances that are surrounding you. The result is that you become helpless and trapped in your circumstances because you have relinquished control and power to outside forces.

I love my parents dearly and do not fault them for raising me the way they did. I believe that God uses everything in our lives if we allow Him to. That is why we are admonished not to hate, to pray for our enemies, love them, and to forgive. This is a tough call, but it has more to do with us and where we are going than the people that have hurt us and the terrible things they had done to us.

When I was growing up, my parents told me and my six other siblings that we should not get married to a foreign woman when the time to get married came. A foreign woman was any woman who was not from the Bamumbu ethnic group. It did not matter if the woman was from Cameroon, my country of birth, or outside of Cameroon. Can you imagine what this means? That other girls born in different ethnic groups in Cameroon may not be good enough for us to get married to.

Before you cast stones on my parents for daring to think like this, I want you to understand that my parents are not the only ones who shared such a sentiment. In Cameroon, inter-ethnic marriages are not commonplace because the Bassas, Ewondos, Bamelike, Bakossi, Bayangi,

Mohgahmos, Balinyongas, Balongs, Bafos, Bakundus, Fulanis, Hausas, Bororos, etc. only want to get married to their own. The few who break these rules are frowned upon. In some cases, families will threaten to disown their children. If you go to Nigeria, the Ibos, Yorubas, Hausas, Fulani, Ibibio, Amasari, Ifik, etc. also prefer to get married to each other. This issue is not limited to West Africa. If you go to East Africa, you will encounter it, even in central Africa and Southern Africa and Northern Africa as well. I dare to make a generalization that in most parts of the world, people from different ethnic groups find it difficult to intermarry, especially when the ethnic groups have a lot of differences.

My parents, just like many other parents who prohibit their children from marrying foreign women, have the best interest of their children at heart. They understand from past experience that interethnic marriage requires more work because of the differences. In some cases, there have been past interethnic wars and the wounds have not healed completely, making it a little difficult for both parties to be united through marriage because marriage is usually not just between two individuals.

Instead of focusing on the challenges that the married couples will face, the parents cross the line when they start using stereotypes and unfounded bias to discourage their children from marrying outside of their ethnic groups. You will be shocked at some of the things parents will tell their children and the great lengths they will go to ensure that their son or daughter does not marry someone from a different ethnic group.

Parents paint the "foreigners" in such a way that this toxin has killed many budding love relationships between people from different ethnic groups. Most parents pride themselves of their language and cultural heritage at the expense of everything else.

Why is it that when a "white family" prohibits their own child from getting married to a person from a different ethnic background, it is blown out of proportion and racism is invoked? Are the concerns of the African parent in any way different? Do some people think what is good for us is not good for others? Do you see how discrimination is a heart issue and found anywhere you have people? If these attitudes are not checked, they will continue to divide the human race.

Some are going to argue that because discrimination is coming from a Caucasian, it is more egregious. I will say whoever thinks like this is refusing to remove the log of wood in their own eye and focusing on the tiny piece of wood in the other person's eye. If you think that disowning and shunning a child because he or she got married to somebody from a different ethnic group is justifiable, you need to wake up.

When I left home and went to the University, it occurred to me that there are subcultures and people who live in a certain city share a lot in common, even if they are from different ethnic groups. Therefore, insisting that one must get married to a woman from one's ethnic group did not make sense. In the past, most of the African ethnic groups were also independent kingdoms. Therefore, getting married across ethnic lines was almost like an international marriage. As I already mentioned, some of these different ethnic groups frequently fought each other, making it difficult for them to intermarry. The issue was that people did not travel far from their place of birth, and everybody remained within their particular ethnic group.

Colonization changed everything, so you will assume. All these different ethnic groups were grouped together to form a country. This led to the emergence of a new economy. For example, plantation agriculture brought people from different ethnic groups to work together. Cities soon sprang up around these plantations, but the ethnic divisions did not die overnight. All these different earth groups still maintained their languages, cultures, and ways of doing things. It must be the lingering fear and mistrust of each other that has prevented total integration. Some of the children born under these new circumstances developed a third culture, and some are intermarrying, but it is not yet the norm. People still prefer to get married to their "own" for various reasons.

I decided to go the other way and got married to a "foreign woman" because we are all human and are not defined by our culture. Love transcends food, clothing, dance, songs, and whatever cultural heritage we may be having. We have sacrificed certain things because we are from two different ethnic groups. For example, we speak English and Pidgin because these are languages that both of us are fluent in, but we cannot speak the languages that belong to our respective ethnic groups.

After getting married, we moved to the United States of America, and for pragmatic reasons, we have encouraged our children to learn

Spanish as a second language because they will use it someday. I had a call from my mum as I was writing this page. She was greeting our first son in the Mundani language, and my son was clueless. She asked him if he did not know what to say, and my son said I had not taught him the language. Well, my son is correct. I have not taught him the language not because there is anything wrong with the language, but because of the sacrifices that one has to make when you migrate to a new country and have a lot of things pulling you left and right. If my wife and I spoke the same language, they would have easily learned it, but we already knew when we were getting married that the English language was common to both of us and it was going to take precedence.

We should not allow fear and ignorance to drive our decision-making process, even when it comes to something as important as marriage. It is important to focus on the fact that the more different your backgrounds are, the more you will have to work on certain areas of the marriage to look for common ground. You don't use unfounded stereotypes and invoke fear of the unknown to discourage people from different ethnic backgrounds from getting married.

Ethnocentrism is alive and well

We discarded the word tribalism for obvious reasons because it is loaded with a lot of baggage that is not helping our efforts to go past mislabeling and mischaracterization of other people. For example, when the Europeans encountered cultures that did not wear clothes, they considered them primitive and backward. I am not saying that nudity should be encouraged, but in these societies where nudity was the norm, you could not sell pornography and nudity because the supply was obviously more than the demand. In western societies, they are now exporting nudity in the form of pornography, and it is a multi-billion dollar industry. There are even communities that insist on going nude in the west. Therefore, to have labeled people who did not have any need for clothing primitive was not well-thought out. We can leave this discussion for another book.

What I am saying is that instead of talking about tribalism, we should focus on ethnocentrism because it is prevalent across the globe, be it among Africans, Chinese, Indians, Hispanics, Caucasians, etc.

The basic question is why is ethnocentrism tolerated when other people engage in it at the exclusion of others, but when the Caucasians manifest it, everybody yells "racism"? This term "racism" has been expanded in the United States of America to mean everybody in the Republican Party and anyone who supports President Trump. This generalization from people who themselves cannot get married to people who are not from their ethnic group and would not allow their children to get married to other children from different ethnic groups is hypocrisy of the highest category and must and should be pointed out.

Why is the idea of Chinatown in the United States of America cool and welcomed while the Caucasians are lambasted for being racist? It is more than shocking the tales of horror and mistreatment you hear from Africans in China and the Middle East. I watched an ad from China and even an exhibit depicting Africans that was too bad that I do not even want to mention it here. Where is the outrage against the Chinese for allowing their ethnocentrism to defile basic human courtesy? What happened to their sensitivity and the dignity of other humans? Is the amount of melanin in somebody's skin the only measure of the person? Whoever thinks like this and behaves like this is ignorant about basic human biology and needs to go get some proper education.

I find it not only hypocritical but lamentable when some people from the Middle East where Christians and people of other faiths are tortured, imprisoned and killed with impunity talk about Americans as racist or people in European countries as racist. These are the same individuals who enjoy all sorts of freedoms in the west that were fought by other people, but they have never pointed a finger against their countries of origin for their barbaric acts against other people in the name of their religion and culture. It is a shame that people who fled oppressive regimes that stifled growth and opportunities move to countries where other people shed their blood and sacrifice all to gain individual freedom and liberty and the best they can contribute is to bring a culture that wants to enslave women and take away the liberty of other people.

Those insisting on introducing and practicing the Sharia law in Western democracies are, in essence, saying that ethnocentrism trumps all. What they care more than anything else is maintaining their way of life because the familiar is safer. If racism were the proper word to describe the actions of these particular individuals, they would be considered the most grievous offenders, to say the least. While they are discriminating against other people, they tend to complain about racism the most. It is not uncommon for them to invoke Islamophobia, but they are not doing enough to let go of their own ways that are in direct conflict with western values and customs. It seems they have forgotten that something good about the west attracted them, and they uprooted themselves from countries where the Sharia law is practiced and the majority of the people embrace it. Obviously, the practice of Sharia law was not working for them, and they decided to go to a better place for a better life. Then, why come to the place and refuse to ask yourself what makes this place different from the one that you left? Why insist on implementing the same ways and customs that did not deliver for you?

All these questions are being asked because you uprooted yourself from your country of birth and moved to a different country because you wanted a better life. If the reason you moved was not for better opportunities but to spread your ideas, conquer and take over, then you should not complain when there is pushback from people in your host country. Unfortunately, we are living in such a "politically correct" world that what I have just written will cost some to call for my head. It seems common sense is dead and has been replaced by irrational emotionalism.

I do not have any score to settle with the Muslims or people who have different religious persuasions, but what I am saying is that if you escape a repressive and oppressive system that prevented you from reaching your full potential, you should, out of a good conscience and character, avoid reestablishing that same system in your new environment. Secondly, you should be vocal about the abuses and excesses of the country of your birth that you fled from. The simple reason being that there are many people back there that are living under oppression and need to be set free.

When you insist on propagating racial superiority in the name of white privilege, you are not solving the problem, but digging a deeper hole for the entire society. After the election of the first biracial president in the history of the United States of America, he talked about racism more than any other president in the history of the country. To say that racism is in the DNA of the United States of America is tantamount to saying that there is no hope for the country. While such a statement scores good political points, it is venom that must be rejected.

Racism is not in the DNA of the United States of America. What each and every human has in them is the propensity to hate, be greedy, lust, lie, cheat, take advantage of others, and commit adultery, you name it. These heart issues are not a respecter of persons and are color blind. You find people who behave like this all over the world and among all ethnicities. The truth is that we are more than flesh and blood and have a spiritual dimension that drives everything else. If this spiritual dimension is not functioning properly, nothing else will.

Most segregated hour in the US

It is Dr. Martin Luther King, Jr. who said, "Sunday morning at 9:00 am is the most segregated hour in the United States of America." Today, you can still hear people throwing this around as proof that racism is in the DNA of the United States of America and that white privilege is true and will never go away. This sentiment does not capture the whole issue.

I will start by saying that racism and Christianity are not supposed to appear in the same sentence because you cannot be a Christian and racist at the same time. There is only one human race, according to the God of the Bible. Therefore, it makes no sense to even think that there is an inferior race that needs to be looked down upon. Let this scripture settle this race issue once and for all. Paul, the apostle, was writing to the church in Rome and here is what he told them:

> *So in Christ Jesus you are all children of God through faith, for all of you who were baptized into Christ have clothed yourselves with Christ. There is neither Jew nor Gentile, neither slave nor free, nor is there male and female, for you are all one in Christ Jesus. If you belong to Christ, then you are Abraham's seed, and heirs according to the promise. Galatians 3:26-29 (NIV)*

Paul was crystal clear here and has declared that we are "all one in Christ Jesus." One means one and any other divisions, no matter how well-intended, are human-driven and not divinely motivated. It is sad that we have to remind Christians to do the right thing and lead the way.

Sunday morning is still highly segregated, and something should be done about it. I am not bringing this up to deepen the racial divide, but to say that this segregation persists because it is two-way traffic. *There is a tendency in all humans to gravitate towards people who look, speak, eat, sing, dance, dress like them, etc.* While there is nothing wrong in being around your own, it is important that in a society that is becoming more and more multi-ethnic, people learn to get out of their "comfort bubbles" and interact with other people. Paul wrote the admonition to remind the church in Rome because they were having some difficulties getting along with each other. God does not expect us to go with the natural flow because we are now children of light and have the God-given capacity to love with divine love. We can no longer continue living as if we have not encountered God.

Contrary to popular feel-good preaching that is being delivered from most pulpits today, God did not send His son to come, suffer, and die on the cross so that we can have a comfortable life. Jesus Christ did not die so that we can join a church and enjoy the type of music, dance, and food that makes us happy. While there is nothing wrong in enjoying good music and being comfortable, it is unacceptable to allow this desire for comfort, the familiar and predictable to distract us from God's mission. The mission of God is simply to reconcile mankind back to Himself. This should take precedence over everything else. It is not happening because the command of Jesus to carry our crosses and follow Him daily is being ignored by many people for obvious reasons. They like to be entertained, taken care of, pampered, and blessed. As long as their needs are being met, nothing else matters. This type of attitude is not of God and should change. It is time the people of God get their act together and lead the way for all the others to follow because we have not been called to be comfortable, but to be light and salt to a dying world.

Segregation on Sunday morning is not restricted to white and black or Asian and Hispanic. You have churches that are made predominantly for people from particular ethnic groups from Africa. For example, some of the churches in the United States may be made up of predominantly people from the Ibo ethnic group or Yoruba. In such churches, the members sing in their ethnic language, pray, and dress accordingly. In other words, they are doing what they are comfortable doing because it is the way they are used to.

You have Korean churches, Chinese, Vietnamese, Burmese, Ethiopian, etc. In fact, most ethnic groups from other parts of the world have their congregations because of the language barrier, cultural sensitivities, and many other personal preferences. Unfortunately, as well intended as these preferences may be, they are not helping the issue of segregation in the country. How can we all work in the corporate world, but when it comes to worshipping God, we start talking about catering to our individual needs.

We have reduced our churches into country clubs were membership has to fit certain criteria. The last time I checked, the command to go make disciples of every nation has not changed. We needed Paul's attitude when he said:

> *Though I am free and belong to no one, I have made myself a slave to everyone, to win as many as possible. To the Jews, I became like a Jew, to win the Jews. To those under the law, I became like one under the law (though I am not under the law), to win those under the law. To those not having the law, I became like one not having the law (though I am not free from God's law but am under Christ's law), to win those not having the law. To the weak, I became weak to win the weak. I have become all things to all people so that by all possible means I might save some. I do all this for the sake of the gospel, that I may share in its blessings. 1 Corinthians 9:19-23 (NIV)*

I pray the day will come when we will put first things first. Prioritizing people's souls above our cultural differences, taste for music, and the type of food we eat at our functions or how the service is conducted are what the church should be doing. Instead, we are more concerned about making people comfortable and accommodating them. If Jesus were only about maintaining the status quo and making people comfortable, He would not have called fishermen and told them that He was going to make them fishers of men. Do you think these fishermen had some apprehension and discomfort for this career change? Paul understood this, and that is why he zoomed in on the need to win souls. The modern church, however, is more concerned about fitting in and going with the flow. The leaders are always careful not to disturb the donor base because they may take their money and leave.

How on earth can immigrants that have moved to the United States of America permanently be encouraged to form their own churches to take care of their own people, instead of integrating? Does the church in the US not see that these brothers and sisters in Christ are here to stay and have to be equipped to be a blessing to the country? It broke my heart when I went to visit a church one Sunday morning and services were being conducted in two separate rooms, one for the Africans by the Africans and the other for the Caucasians by the Caucasians. Whoever thinks this is the brightest and greatest idea to do ministry is sacrificing the future of the country and the purpose of the kingdom of God on the altar of convenience. This thinking has to be challenged and changed because it is not Biblical, and it is supporting and reinforcing the stereotypes that are already out there.

One of my pastor friends from Cameroon who has an African church in Dallas told me that he was told to start in his Jerusalem, implying that he has to reach out to the Cameroonian community in the Dallas area.

First of all, why are we talking about a Cameroonian Community in the United States of America when all these Cameroonians are American citizens or soon-to-become citizens? Some of these individuals are happy to be hyphenated Americans, for example, Nigerian-American, Cameroonian-American, Ethiopian-American, Indian-American, etc.

Why is just being an American not good enough? Most of the immigrants left their countries of origin, but these countries did not leave them. They want to eat their cake and still want to have it. How can America, which has been such a blessing to you, not be good enough for you to put her first? Most of these immigrants form organizations that cater only to their needs and are not even open to other American citizens or people from other ethnic groups to join. Most of these organizations bear the names of the particular ethnic groups to which these immigrants belonged. For example, there are hundreds of organizations that represent the different ethnic groups from Cameroon. Theses organization ensure that these different ethnic groups maintain their cultures and other practices that they engaged in while they were in their countries of birth.

There is nothing wrong for any ethnic group to maintain their culture, but at what price? When people from other countries exclude other people from their organization because of ethnocentrism, you do not hear any cries of racism, but it seems to be accepted that people from other cultures in the United States of America can discriminate based on cultural difference. Why do these different ethnic groups not form organizations that are open to all other people to become members? The reason people give is that they do not want to lose their culture. However, if the group is trying to maintain their culture at the expense of national unity, the United States of America is going to become weaker and weaker with each passing year because people are no longer going to be having allegiance to the country, but to their particular ethnic group.

The end result will cause havoc, which is what is happening in many different parts of the world where divisions are fueled by ethnocentrism. For example, when one particular ethnic group gains political power, they ensure their firm grip on power. They discriminate against all the other ethnic groups by staffing people from their ethnic group in positions of power. In these countries, opportunities to advance economically are restricted because preferential treatment is given to those with political power.

One of the most common complaint you hear about Africa is ethnocentrism, which some people call tribalism. This ethnocentrism breeds corruption and rampant mismanagement that has caused hundreds of thousands to flee the continent for better opportunities elsewhere. I was listening to Professor Patric Lumumba, the outspoken anti-corruption advocate in Africa, and he said that even in the church in Africa "the blood of ethnicity is thicker than the blood of Jesus Christ." We, as followers of Jesus Christ, are supposed to put aside our ethnic differences, preferences, and loyalties for the sake of the gospel and unity in the body of Christ. Unfortunately, the opposite is true because many professing to be Christians prefer people from their own ethnic group over all others.

It is very common from various ethnicities in the United States of America to accuse other people of racism when their own actions are not any different.

To get rid of racism, it is going to require the society to recognize that the tendency to discriminate against other people is not restricted to just the interaction between whites and blacks, but the interaction between all people.

Chapter 4:
Lessons from the Past

We cannot change the past, only recover from it. And perhaps learn its cruel lessons. Dan Pena

You may be thinking that I am giving a pass to all the perpetrators of racism and those that have seized native lands, exploited, enslaved, and pillaged other cultures. Those advocating for social justice and calling for reparations for past crimes are not looking at the complete picture because they are making sweeping generalizations about the past that are not so. I strongly condemn whatever happened in the past and may still be happening. In the same light, anybody in this day and age who still thinks that the amount of melanin in somebody's skin is a great criterion to divide humans into different races should wake up. In addition, anybody who thinks melanin, which is meant to protect people from the sun's radiation, is some sort of a flaw or handicap that justifies them to look down on other people needs to come down from their high horse and face reality. The color of somebody's skin has nothing whatsoever to do with intellectual capacity, integrity, worth, and achievement.

Therefore, anybody who thinks that they can justify their hate, discrimination, and maltreatment of other people because of their skin color is the one that needs help the most and should seek help as soon as possible. Skin color does not make some people superior and others inferior. Can you point to any reputable scientific journal that has any peer-review study that supports such absurdity? You may be insisting that you heard or watched some movie or read some book that said such and such about other ethnicities. All those sources are wrong because they will not stand the scrutiny when facts are engaged.

While I have zero tolerance for those who believe that skin color is some reliable criterion to classify and discriminate against people, I will differ in the way forward. The purpose of writing this book is not to fan hate and intolerance because anybody who goes down the road of hate and vengeance are subjecting themselves in the worst kind of slavery. It is almost better to be in physical chains than to be mentally bound.

Yes, the past is too dark and painful and the present is equally disheartening. However, it will be a tragedy to allow other people to control not only your past, but your present and your future. Just because people believed in the past and acted as if they were superior to those of a different skin color is not enough to continue to blame and reinforce this viewpoint. Those who believed that they were superior were wrong and are still wrong, but it takes somebody to accept that they are inferior for this insanity to continue. It is time to stand tall in the truth and declare it with all conviction. All men are created equal. Period! This is the truth that will set both the oppressed and the oppressor free because both of them need to be liberated.

We must be extremely cautious and should move slowly and meticulously when trying to use present circumstances to judge the past. When things are taken out of context, there is a tendency to cause more harm than good.

Most of the challenges that we are dealing with today have been dealt with in the past. Therefore, we may do ourselves a lot of good if we take a look at how some people handled maltreatment, social injustice, and slavery.

While some may dismiss these stories and experiences as mere stories, I invite you to take a close look and appreciate the powerful message of hope that is embedded in these powerful narratives.

The case of Joseph

What happened to Joseph, the 11th son of Jacob was despicable, unacceptable, and troubling because it was conceived and executed by his own brothers. If some stranger had done it, one would have had some understanding. For brothers to rise up against their brother and sell him to a foreign country as a slave because they were jealous of him is a prime indication of what issues of the heart can do.

Joseph was known for all the wonderful dreams that predicted that he was going to be a leader and greater than his brothers. These dreams did not sit well with his brothers, and they developed hatred towards him.

To make matters worse, Joseph was daddy's boy and received special favors from their father, Jacob. Joseph would also report about his brothers to their father. Their hatred for Joseph grew to the point where they considered killing him.

One day, they had their opportunity. Jacob sent Joseph to go and give supplies to his brothers. When his brothers saw him coming from afar, they decided that when he arrives, they were going to kill him and all his dreams as well.

When Joseph arrived, his brothers immediately arrested him and threw him into a dry water well. They held a meeting to determine his fate. The decision was to kill him, but one brother suggested that they sell him as a slave to Egypt. The reasoning was that Joseph will be as good as dead if sold as a slave and they will make some money out of it. His brothers were so sure that Joseph was going to die. When they went home, they told their father that Joseph was dead and even showed his coat that was torn and covered in blood. They had killed a goat and smeared Joseph's special coat with the blood. Can you imagine the length these brothers went to eliminate their brother? What were they thinking? We have already shown that the issues of the heart drive people's actions, not their circumstances. These brothers were driven by jealousy, anger, and hatred for Joseph, and the result is that they "killed" him and were not ashamed to tell their father that he was dead.

Joseph was deprived of his father's love, the comfort of his home, and all of his dreams by none other than his own flesh and blood. His brothers sold him to slave traders who took him to Egypt and sold him to another master. It was not enough to be sold the first time, he had to be resold. Can you imagine the trauma Joseph went through as he was chained and yanked off to Egypt? He was in a foreign country among people who had little regard for Hebrews. He was put to work by his owner, and it is reported that Joseph excelled at the task he was given to do because God was with him. Because of his hard work, Joseph was promoted to be in charge of all his master's businesses.

The mistress took notice of Joseph and wanted to have sex with him. He refused because he did not want to sin before God. Here was a slave who had no right to say no to his owner, but feared God enough to know who was his true owner. Joseph could have slept with his master's wife and justified it by saying as a slave, he was supposed to obey orders because he had zero rights. Joseph understood that people could claim that they were his owners and even treated him as such and hold him captive, but his true owner was God, and that is the person to whom he was ultimately accountable. While Joseph was a slave, he was still free because he refused to allow sin to control his life.

His act of disobedience and defiance to his mistress "backfired" on Joseph because this woman was so evil that she lied about him to her husband. Joseph had his own #MeToo moment when this woman told her husband that Joseph had tried to rape her, and after struggling with him, he had run out of the bedroom, leaving his cloak behind. Of course, this was a made-up story. After repeated failed attempts to seduce Joseph, the opportune moment presented itself. On this particular day, this woman realized that the house was empty and Joesph was in the house doing his normal chores. She grabbed him and tried to pull him to the bed with her. This was a desperate attempt on her part to physically achieve what her seductive words failed to do. But Joseph was not going to have any of it, and in the process of struggling to free himself from her grip, she pulled his cloak, and he ran out of the room without it.

When her husband came back, she had Exhibit A, and nobody could dispute her story of attempted rape by Joseph. The judgment was swift, and the penalty was served. Joseph was immediately thrown into prison without any possibility of parole and no indication that he was ever going to be released. This woman had framed him up and was about to finish what his brothers had started, that is, to put an end to all his dreams of rising up to prominence. This was the end of his life, and there was no appeal because he was a slave that had done a despicable act.

Can you imagine how Joseph must have felt after being falsely accused, wrongly convicted, and then imprisoned? Maybe he thought that if his brothers had not been so hateful towards him and his dreams, he would still be home with his father. If his brothers had not sold him into slavery, he would not have encountered this evil woman who has caused him to be imprisoned for a crime he had not committed.

What on earth was God thinking by letting this woman, who had accused him falsely, go free? Where was justice when he needed it most? How could he obey God, and instead of being rewarded, He allowed him to be sent unjustly to prison where there was no hope for him ever escaping? This was a death sentence on all the dreams that he had been shown before this encounter.

It is extremely important to understand that everything was stacked against Joseph at this point, and there was no way humanly speaking that his dreams were going to be realized. Not only was he a slave, but he was also in prison with no hope of getting out. Even if he was liberated from the prison, he was still going to be a slave in a land where slaves were looked down upon. No matter how you look at it, Joseph was in a helpless situation, and only a miracle was going to change his circumstances.

In prison, Joseph did not allow himself to be distracted or depressed. He understood that a person can be imprisoned physically, but the worst prison is that of the mind. He knew God was still with him, and he did so well that he was placed in charge of all the other prisoners by the chief guard. He did not dwell on his misfortune or allow the fact that he had been wrongly condemned to that prison.

One morning, it was reported that Joseph saw one of the prisoners was downcast and sorrowful. Apparently, he had a cheerful countenance because no depressed person ever tries to help another depressed person. Joseph forgot about his own troubles for a moment and reached out to his fellow prisoner.

It turned out that he used to be a high-ranking official in the court of Pharoah and had fallen out of favor with the king. Whatever he had done must have been so bad that the king sent him to prison. Here was a former cupbearer of Pharaoh who had tasted what it meant to be in a position of power, influence, and privilege. He was so depressed that Joseph, a slave, was the one consoling him. The cupbearer was perplexed because he had a troubling dream the night before and was trying to figure out what it meant.

In his dream, the cupbearer had been released from prison and was restored to his former duties as a cupbearer to Pharaoh. After Joseph listened to this man, he assured him that it was God who gave interpretations to dreams. Joseph told him that in three days, this man was going to be released from prison and restored to his position. The interpretation sounded good because it was a positive one.

While they were talking, another prisoner was listening nearby carefully and intently. He, too, used to be the chief baker of Pharoah. This former baker had been thrown in prison for some reason that is not mentioned in the story, and he, too, had a dream that was making him depressed. In the dream, he was carrying a big basket containing a lot of different baked goods, and the birds landed on the basket and ate the baked goods.

The former baker shared his dream with Joseph expecting a positive outcome, just like the cupbearer. Unfortunately for this man, he was going to be released after three days and will be hanged and the birds will eat his body. This was not the outcome that he expected. It is amazing that Joseph was not afraid to tell this man nothing but the truth about his situation. Can you imagine what would have happened if Joseph allowed political correctness to get in his way? He would have told this man what the man wanted to hear, but this would have eroded Joseph's integrity and credibility as somebody who could interpret dreams.

After two years, Pharaoh himself had two dreams that troubled his heart when he got up one morning, but there was nobody in the entire land of Egypt that could interpret his dreams. After a frantic search and failed attempt to find anybody that could interpret the dreams, the cupbearer who was in prison with Joseph remembered him, and this is what he said:

Then the chief cupbearer said to Pharaoh, "Today, I am reminded of my shortcomings. Pharaoh was once angry with his servants, and he imprisoned me and the chief baker in the house of the captain of the guard. Each of us had a dream the same night, and each dream had a meaning of its own. Now a young

Hebrew was there with us, a servant of the captain of the guard. We told him our dreams, and he interpreted them for us, giving each man the interpretation of his dream. And things turned out exactly as he interpreted them to us: I was restored to my position, and the other man was impaled." Genesis 41: 9-13 (NIV)

It is not a coincidence that the cupbearer talked about Joseph confidently because Joseph had a track record that could be verified. Had Joseph allowed his feelings and preferences to influence how he interpreted the dreams, he would not have been called to come to interpret Pharaoh's dreams. I am pointing this out because Joseph had every reason not to maintain his integrity because his circumstances were not comfortable. But he allowed what was on the inside to take the upperhand and this opened unprecedented doors for him. It is reported that immediately upon hearing how Joseph had successfully interpreted other dreams in the past, the Pharaoh did the following:

So Pharaoh sent for Joseph, and he was quickly brought from the dungeon. When he had shaved and changed his clothes, he came before Pharaoh. Genesis 41: 14 (NIV)

Suddenly, Joseph was the talk of the town because he was freed from prison and went on to become the second strongest man in the whole of Egypt. After successfully interpreting the Pharaoh's dream, he was made the prime minister of Egypt. His dream had come true. He had power and influence. He had the power of life and death in his hands.

Then, the unthinkable happened. Joseph's brothers showed up hungry and desperate for food. There was famine in the land, and they needed food for their families, and Joseph was in charge of selling food. Was this the right time to punish his brothers for all they had done to him? Was it payback time?

Before Joseph made himself known to his brothers, he invited them to his house to have a meal with him. Remember, it was mentioned that the Egyptians discriminated against the Hebrews. Because when Joseph invited his brothers, they had to eat by themselves according to the following account:

They served him by himself, the brothers by themselves, and the Egyptians who ate with him by themselves because Egyptians could not eat with Hebrews, for that is detestable to Egyptians. Genesis 43:32 (NIV)

Can you imagine how ethnocentric the Egyptians were? They considered the Hebrews detestable to the point where they would not even eat with them. This is a prime example of discrimination at work. Joseph had been a slave, was treated badly and discriminated against. He was able to rise up to the occasion and overcome this discrimination because he provided a solution to Egypt in her hour of greatest need. Pharoah's dream had predicted seven years of abundance in the entire land of Egypt to be followed by seven years of famine. The famine was going be so severe that people will completely forget the years of abundance. They needed solutions on what to do, and Joseph provided a solution that propelled him to the top. The Egyptians had to swallow their pride and disdain for Hebrews by allowing this Hebrew slave to become the second most powerful person in the entire country. This is a profound lesson that all who want to make a difference should learn. Instead of complaining and grumbling how you are being treated, you should be focusing on how to provide solutions. When people provide solutions, doors will open, and their situation will change.

I consider this one of the most tense, yet profound teachable moments in the entire Bible. Joseph wanted to inquire from his brothers about their father and the rest of the family, this is what transpired:

Then Joseph could no longer control himself before all his attendants, and he cried out, "Have everyone leave my presence!" So there was no one with Joseph when he made himself known to his brothers. And he wept so loudly that the Egyptians heard him, and Pharoah's household heard about it. Genesis 45:1-2 (NIV)

Joseph decided to send out everybody because he did not want to disgrace his brothers. It was a family affair, and there was no need for them to "wash their dirty linens in public." It is amazing that instead of blaming his brothers, ridiculing them or pointing an accusatory finger against them and demanding justice, Joseph wept! He created the privacy that was needed for such an event to let his brothers know that they were safe and that whatever had transpired in the past will and has not been wasted.

The following verse captures precisely what one would have expected from his brothers because they were guilty as charged, and the evil they had done to their brother had not left them. But Joseph had other ideas in mind. He was on a completely different dimension from his brothers. While his brothers were focusing on the past, Joseph was looking at what is yet to come and how the past is guaranteeing that glorious future. This is what gave him the courage to draw his brothers closer instead of disgracing them in public.

> *Joseph said to his brothers, "I am Joseph! Is my father still living?" But his brothers were not able to answer him, because they were terrified at his presence. Genesis 45:3 (NIV)*

His brothers were in total shock and disbelief because they could not understand how a slave had become the second most powerful person in the most powerful country in the world at that time. In addition, the guilt from what they had done to their brother surfaced and it must have been unbearable. To make matters worse, Joseph had the power of life and death over them, and they knew it. Before this, Joseph had asked one of them to be placed in prison and they were helpless in defending their brother.

Joseph did not wait for his brothers who had wronged him to speak or ask for forgiveness or even plead for their lives. Instead, he forgave his brothers without any precondition or demands. What followed are some of the most beautiful words in the entire Bible:

> *Then Joseph said to his brothers, "Come close to me." When they had done so, he said, "I am your brother Joseph, the one you sold into Egypt!* ***And now, do not be distressed and do not be angry with yourselves for selling me here because it was to save lives that God sent me ahead of you.*** *For two years now, there has been famine in the land, and for the next five years there will be no plowing and reaping. But God sent me ahead of you to preserve for you a remnant on earth and to save your lives by a great deliverance.*

"So then, it was not you who sent me here, but God. He made me father to Pharaoh, lord of his entire household and ruler of all Egypt. Genesis 45:4-8 (NIV)

There is so much in these few verses that it will take many books to digest it. Can you imagine what is going on here? Joseph had the power to destroy his brothers who sold him into slavery and caused him to suffer for 13 years, but refused to use that power to seek revenge from his brothers. Instead, he said that they should not be angry for selling him. What was Joseph thinking by letting these criminals go free? Then, he did the unthinkable by completely vindicating his brothers with the following statement:

"So then, it was not you who sent me here, but God."

Joseph was acting weird here. Not only was he delusional in offering the olive branch to his brothers and forgiving them even though they did not ask for his forgiveness, he was saying that his brothers did not commit the very crime they admitted to committing and were even terrified of it. In fact, before they had this encounter with Joseph, the brothers had said among themselves that God may be punishing them for what they did to their brother. Was Joseph out of his mind by suggesting that his brothers had not done anything wrong and that they should not be distressed for selling him? What was he saying here? Why bring God's name into this mess?

A few things about Joseph

I want to reiterate that the life of Joseph has so much to teach us on how to navigate the toxic environment we are currently living in. There are too many lessons in his life that if we learn and apply even one of them, racism will not only be defeated — it will be eradicated for good.

As you can tell by now, I am fascinated by Joseph's life and have drawn a lot of inspiration from him. While other people blame him for sharing his dreams with his brothers, I blame his brothers for allowing anger and jealousy to take over their lives. It is sad that his brothers did not see the big picture and could not predict what was going to happen in the future, and got envious because their brother could.

Here are a few things that set Joseph apart and anybody who can apply these principles in their lives will triumph over racism and any other thing that may be thrown at them.

1. Fear of God and obedience to His laws

Before Joseph was even sold to Egypt, he reported about his brother's misconduct to their father. This is an indication that Joseph was God-fearing from childhood. No wonder when he was tempted in Egypt by his master's wife, he refused to allow his feelings or circumstances to lead him. Nobody would have blamed a slave that got seduced by his owner because he was not expected to say no. But Joseph understood what King Solomon will say a few thousand years later concerning committing adultery:

My son, pay attention to my wisdom,

turn your ear to my words of insight,

that you may maintain discretion

and your lips may preserve knowledge.

For the lips of the adulterous woman drip honey,

and her speech is smoother than oil;

but in the end she is bitter as gall,

sharp as a double-edged sword.

Her feet go down to death;

her steps lead straight to the grave.

She gives no thought to the way of life;

her paths wander aimlessly, but she does not know it. Proverbs 5:1-6 (NIV)

Committing adultery is not only a sin against God but against oneself. How many people do you know throughout history that have been ruined by adultery? Joesph would have ruined his dreams if he fell into this trap. Even though he was young and had sexual needs, he refused to let his needs trump God's law. How many people today disobey God's law just because it feels good, or they have the desire to do whatever their body tells them to do? If you dare to warn them of the harm they are bringing on themselves, you will be accused of passing judgment. This is not true because God's laws are not generated by any of us. The laws are given for our good, and when we break them, we will suffer the consequences.

You may be wondering what fearing God and obeying his laws have to do with racism and the excesses of ethnocentricism. The connection is that if you have a disregard for God's law in one area, you will not necessarily obey God's law in other areas. Joseph was able to forgive his brothers because first he understood that forgiveness is mandated, just as not committing adultery is. Therefore, learning how to resist the temptation to commit adultery empowered Joseph to forgive his brothers.

2. Forgiveness

I already mentioned that all have sinned and need forgiveness. Joseph understood this, and it helped him to see beyond his brothers' egregious offense. What this brother did was despicable, but it was not beyond forgiveness. Consider what Jesus Christ taught us about forgiving one another. His disciples had come to him, asking him to teach them how to pray. Jesus taught them what we now call the Lord's Prayer, and part of it is the request for God to forgive us. Then Jesus added the following instructions concerning forgiveness:

> *For if you forgive other people when they sin against you, your heavenly Father will also forgive you. But if you do not forgive others their sins, your Father will not forgive your sins. Matthew 6:14-15 (NIV)*

Without forgiveness, none of us has any hope, including those trapped in the superiority and inferiority complexes that are branded as racism. People have been hurt, and some hurt very badly. Nobody can say that a lot of damage and senseless killings, pillaging and terrible atrocities have not been committed under the disguise of racism. While all these heinous and despicable acts perpetuated and carried out are painful, discouraging, and plain evil, we must force ourselves as Joseph did to see the hand of God amid all this pain and choose the high road of forgiveness.

You may be saying, "But it is painful, and it seems the perpetrators are walking free when they must be punished." Here is where you may be wrong in thinking that you know how to punish somebody for their crimes. Only God can dish out the punishment that each person deserves, and you must trust God to execute that punishment. The brothers of Joseph were so guilty that years later, after their father died, they went to their brother and pleaded for their lives. Can you imagine the torture and mental anguish these brothers went through during their lives? Please do not try to be God because that is something that you are not cut out for. Instead, follow the admonition in the word of God:

Beloved, do not avenge yourselves, but rather give place to wrath; for it is written, "Vengeance is Mine, I will repay," says the Lord. Romans 12:19 (NKJV)

Repay no one evil for evil. Have regard for good things in the sight of all men. Romans 12:17 (NKJV)

Do not say, "I will do to him just as he has done to me;

I will render to the man according to his work." Proverbs 24:29 (NKJV)

Forgiveness is a command, and if you do not forgive, you are jeopardizing your own soul. This is something that Joseph understood and acted upon because he understood that letting go of hate and vengeance was good for him. He trusts God to take care of his brothers. Many people are calling for payback and stirring up emotions and replaying what happened in the past or are happening right now. If we are not careful, we will take the bait and enslave ourselves. While we acknowledge that great harm has been done, we should not try to overcome evil with evil because that does not work. We must overcome evil with good because light always displaces darkness.

You may be thinking that the perpetrators have hurt you or your people too many times and there is no way you are going to forgive them because they have overdone it.

Peter thought like that when he asked Jesus the following. The question came up because a servant who owed his master, let's say, a million dollars, pleaded for his master to forgive the debt, and his master did. Then, this servant turned around and held another servant who owed him one hundred dollars. Not only did this servant insist on being paid, he actually threw the other servant in prison. Word got to their master because other servants went and reported the ungrateful servant to their master. The master threw the ungrateful servant in prison and insisted that he had to pay off all his debt before he is released.

This situation troubled Peter, and when they were alone with Jesus, it is written

Then Peter came to Him and said, "Lord, how often shall my brother sin against me, and I forgive him? Up to seven times?"

Jesus said to him, "I do not say to you, up to seven times, but up to seventy times seven. Matthew 18:21-22 (NKJV)

The command to forgive is crystal clear here, and there is no limit to how many times you should forgive on a given day. The bottom line is that all of us have received unlimited mercy from God and should extend it to other people. This is something that Joseph understood, believed in, and acted upon. We, too, should learn how to forgive.

Here is a warning from great contemporary leaders, two of whom were murdered and one who served 27 years in prison for standing up against discrimination. These men did not only talk the talk, but they also walked the talk, and we can learn a lot from them.

"Darkness cannot drive out darkness; only light can do that. Hate cannot drive out hate; only love can do that." Martin Luther King, Jr.

"The weak can never forgive. Forgiveness is the attribute of the strong." Mahatma Gandhi

"If there are dreams about a beautiful South Africa, there are also roads that lead to their goal. Two of these roads could be named Goodness and Forgiveness." Nelson Mandela

If after all this, you still think walking in hate and vengeance is the way to go, consider the words of Marianne Williamson, "Unforgiveness is like drinking poison yourself and waiting for the other person to die."

Each time God prohibits us from doing anything, it is because He wants to protect us from harm. At times, those calling for social justice sanctify hate, unforgiveness, and vengeance. This toxic concoction is wrapped in social justice, and many people drink this harmful Kool-Aid, and it destroys them. There is nothing more destructive to an individual and eventually, a society than harboring anger, bitterness, and unforgiveness. These will destroy anybody who allows them to take hold in their heart. Therefore, you should flee away from anger, hate, unforgiveness, and vengeance and make up your mind to choose the higher road, choose light, and say no to unforgiveness.

3. Understanding the bigger picture

Joseph understood who was the true master and who had the final say and the ultimate plan. This is why even though he was a slave, he refused to obey his mistress to commit adultery.

He was following a bigger plan: the plan God had revealed to Abraham many years before Joseph was born. God had promised that Abraham's descendants were going down to Egypt and be enslaved, but they will be delivered and brought back to possess the promised land. In short, God wanted them to get to Egypt to become a critical mass so that they can come back and occupy the land.

Abraham passed this promise to Isaac, who passed it to Jacob, who passed it to Joseph and his brothers. Apparently, only Joseph understood what was going on. God had given Joseph some dreams, but these dreams were not to promote him, but part of God's redemption plan. This is why Joseph attributed his being sold to Egypt a divine act and not his brothers betraying him.

4. Living above your circumstances

Joseph was enslaved, but his spirit was free because he refused to obey the dictates of the wife of his owner. Although one would have expected Joseph to comply because he was owned and had no right to say no, he understood who the true master was. The person calling the shots was God, that is why it is recorded that God was with him both in Potiphar's house and in prison. Even in prison, Joseph did not allow himself to be depressed; he still excelled because God was with him. Joseph understood that with God in control, his circumstances were not supposed to take charge.

Many people blame their circumstances and other people for why they are not doing well. This attitude will keep you grounded for life. When you allow other people and your circumstances to take the upper hand in your life, you have relinquished control and will become trapped in a prison of your own making. This is the type of prison that is almost impossible to escape from because you have locked the door and thrown away the keys. Do not allow your circumstances or what other people have done to you to become your reality. There is always another reality — the God reality. Knowing that God is with you no matter what is more than anything else. With God on your side, you can never be defeated. All the momentary setbacks are just launching pads and stepping stones to better things.

5. Making the most with what you have

Your gift will make a way for you no matter what your circumstances are or what other people think about you or do to you. Therefore, it is more important to find out what your gift is and start using it, instead of complaining about your circumstances. Joseph had the gift of interpreting dreams, and he used it while in prison. Remember that he was falsely accused, wrongfully convicted, and imprisoned. He could have allowed anger and bitterness to prevent him from making use of his gift. Instead, he cared about the other prisoners enough to reach out and help them.

Every person has a unique gift that they are born with, and it is your responsibility to discover this gift and use it to render service to other people. No matter where you are and what you are going through, your gift, when used in the right way, will make a way for you. Joseph did not wait to be freed from prison to use his gift; in fact, using his gift while in prison became the key that opened the prison doors and set him free. Do you know what your own gift is? Are you using it, or have you allowed your past to run your present and steal your future?

Now is your opportunity to put things in perspective by engaging your community with your gift. All other yokes and bondages will be broken. You can be free even in prison because freedom transcends the physical barrier. If you refuse to use your gift, you are placing yourself in the worst prison imaginable because nobody can set you free from such a prison except you.

Your gift will bring you before kings

There is nothing wrong with setting up advocacy groups to fight for the rights of others. The call for social justice and equality sounds great and it is highly necessary, but this alone will not do it. Government intervention and laws are great, but all laws are limited because a lot depends on the individual and what they do with their gift.

Please do not get me wrong. If all we needed were more and better laws, the issue of segregation and discrimination would have been eradicated a long time ago. Justice and equality would have been achieved, and all of us will be living in peace and harmony. While most countries have good laws and excellent programs, the heart of the issue is the need for a change of heart from all parties involved.

One sure way to get equality is not through mandated government regulations. Individuals must find their gifts and start using them. We are not a cosmic accident we were created and endowed with unique gifts that are designed to get us to the top. Joseph understood this very well and exemplified it. There was no advocacy group fighting for his release and nobody was calling for social justice, but his gift of interpreting dreams came to his rescue because he used it. I have already stated he could have allowed his circumstances to discourage him, but he chose to use his gift. You, too, must stop complaining and start using your gift.

The shortcut to prominence is by solving problems

Joseph did not become the number two in Egypt because somebody pitied him or advocated for him to be given that job. Remember that the Egyptians detested the Hebrews and they would not even eat with them. This is discrimination at its worst. Nobody set up a committee to fight against this discrimination, but when Joseph cared enough for others to meet their needs, he was positioned to become the number two most powerful person in Egypt.

It has been said that the cream will always rise to the top. When you focus on the needs of others, you will be inspired with solutions to meet those needs. Unfortunately, many people are so wrapped up in their own issues that they have no time to think about other people. The way to get to the top is by solving other people's problems.

Remember that Joseph was sold by his brothers and thrown in prison, but he did not allow all this mistreatment and injustice to get him depressed and self-centered. Instead, he deployed his gift to serve Potiphar. It made his business flourish; in prison, he used his gift to serve other people.

When the time came that there was a need to point out what direction Egypt had to go, Joseph was called up because he had a track record of using his gift to solve problems for other people. He was doing this even when his circumstances were far from ideal or comfortable.

What problems are you solving? What needs are you meeting? You must discover your gift and deploy it to serve others. When you provide solutions, your background, socioeconomic status, and skin color will not count. Therefore, to gain true freedom, start by identifying your gift and use it to solve problems. Nothing will stop you from getting to the top if you are a problem-solver. Unfortunately, many people will rather complain, complain, and neglect their gift because they think other people have power over them.

With God on your side, you are the majority

Joseph did not need the approval of his brothers when he decided to report their misconduct to their father. There was no need for Joseph to go along with the other 10 brothers' behavior. We live in a time where there is great pressure for us to fit in and be just like everyone else. Whatever is trending, you have to get along, even if it is against the law of God. This is not the way to gain your freedom and experience the best that God has for you. It is better for you to be with God than be with the crowd. As the life of Joseph demonstrated, when God is with you, He is always going to make a way for you no matter what.

If you think it is just a coincidence that a slave in one of the most repressive societies rose up to become the second most powerful person in the country, you are mistaken because without God's involvement in Joseph's life, he would not have overcome all the adversities that befell him.

You can rise above institutionalized discrimination

One of the biggest complaints of people living in societies where discrimination is institutionalized and has become the law of the land is how impossible it is to rise above. They rightfully talk about the lack of access to jobs, opportunities, healthcare, and upward social mobility. People of "color" are unlikely to be appointed to occupy a certain position. In some countries, if you are from a minority ethnic group, you can never occupy certain positions.

It is not easy to overcome institutionalized discrimination, but Joseph's life demonstrates that it is possible. Instead of focusing on what is being done against you and all the roadblocks that you have to overcome, focus on discovering your gift and perfecting it. As idealistic as this may sound, this is the only hope that we have to defeat such hatred, ignorance, and bigotry. You cannot win this war by complaining and letting the action of others push you into anger and self-pity.

Joseph had every opportunity to complain about the Egyptian society, the discrimination, and the oppression of slaves that was entrenched in that society. He could have bemoaned the lack of opportunities and upward social mobility, but he chose to focus on what he could bring to the table. He focused on what he had, not what he didn't have. This approach is counterintuitive, but therein lies the true power for holistic transformation. When we focus on doing what we can and get better at it, eventually, doors will open. It takes time and a lot of work to get good at what you have been ordained to do. Part of the issue we have today is that most people believe the wrong things about them and as a result, blame other people for their predicament. When individuals begin to walk in the truth by rejecting the lies that have been fed to them, about who they are and what they can or cannot do, nothing—not even institutionalized discrimination—will be able to stop them.

If you doubt what I just said, ask Nelson Mandela who, after 27 years in prison, oversaw the dismantling of an oppressive apartheid regime that believed dark-skinned South Africans could not participate in government, even though they were the majority of the population.

There is one other thing that enabled Joseph to overcome institutionalized discrimination in Egypt. It is written:

> *By faith, Joseph, when he was dying, made mention of the departure of the children of Israel, and gave instructions concerning his bones. Hebrews 11:22 (NKJV)*

Joseph was a person of faith, and this enabled him to see the future. This unique perspective of seeing the bigger picture meant that Joseph was able to see through the present limitations that were surrounding him.

Without faith, love, and hope, we are all doomed because these are the qualities that can change hearts and keep us going, even when the hearts have not yet been changed. While it is important and necessary to dismantle institutionalized discrimination, you do not have to wait for this to happen for you to walk in your calling.

Joseph understood that being in Egypt was not the final destination and that God had a bigger and better plan. Do you see the bigger picture? There are many things about your life that you had no control over, and it is going to take faith in God for you to understand how to navigate your way forward. For example, you did not choose your parents, when and where to be born. You were not consulted about the color of your skin or the social class in which you were born. Therefore, do not let anybody tell you that any of these things that you did not choose can stop you. The things that can stop you are the choices you make and what you believe about yourself and your abilities.

Have faith that God will perfect His plan for your life by making use of you as you are. You do not need to change your ethnicity or skin color to fulfill your destiny. This is ground zero if you want to rise above institutionalized discrimination.

Change yourself, not others

Apart from the incident of Joseph telling his brothers about their misdeeds, there is nowhere that he tried to change other people. The dreams he had were about him and his future, although his brothers were mentioned in them, he did not make the dreams about them. In Egypt, when his master's wife tried to seduce him, he did not tell her that she should change. He told her that he could not commit such a sin against God. In other words, Joseph was focused on his role and responsibility. He did not try to force his master to stop being a slave owner. This is not to say that there is anything wrong in fighting to free people from slavery and other forms of unfair servitude.

What you should be paying attention here to is the tendency for some to resort to name calling and hurling insults that do not change anything. Instead of saying that "They did this to me and therefore, they should become such and such," say "I am better than what they did to me and above where they have placed me." Don't wait for those who believe that they are superior to you to change before you believe that you are not inferior. I cannot stress this enough. Just because somebody believes that your skin color makes you inferior and treats you as if you are inferior does not mean that you have to believe it.

Never allow the opinions of others about you to become your reality. If somebody says that you are a donkey and treats you like a donkey, will you accept?

Are you a donkey because somebody believes that you are a donkey and passes laws that clearly state that you are a donkey?

What you believe is what will rule over you. All people are created equal. If there is an alternative, please share with me.

It is the truth that sets people free, not the traditions and cultural norms that are not based on facts!

When did the amount of melanin in somebody's skin become a base for defining that person? Can you determine the quality of the house solely on the paint on the exterior of the house?

Stop believing and spreading this craziness. Is it not written that we are all one in Christ? One human race, created in the image of God. Who do you believe? Let God be true, and all others are liars!

Focus on changing you, not the other person who has chosen to believe a lie and live in ignorance. If all the facts about the human race have not convinced somebody to realize that skin color is not enough to segregate us, then you might as well allow that person to wallow in their ignorance. Allow them to feel superior all they want because it is a figment of their imagination. However, if you dare believe that you are in any way inferior, a victim or in a disadvantageous position, then you are feeding this monster, and it will eat you up.

Please resist the temptation to resort to anger, resentment, and bitterness because these feelings can put you in a self-imposed prison that you may never escape. If you allow love to guide you, nobody is going to trample on you. I did not say they will not try to, but when they do, they will fail. They will only succeed if you believe they will. Therefore, focus on changing your belief system. This is something that I am going to dwell on in the last chapter.

The slave masters prevented the slaves from reading and writing because they knew that reading was going to expose the slaves to the truth, and once people know the truth, it will set them free. How about you? What books are you reading? What are you feeding your mind with? Do you know that you become your thoughts? Nobody controls your thoughts but you. Whatever you think about happens eventually.

Many people want to keep blaming others because they do not want to take responsibility for their actions. You are not obliged to accept whatever status people give you or whatever name they give you. It is your responsibility to refuse to be a second-class citizen, even if other people insist that you are. Blaming, complaining, and refusing to do your part will fail and has always failed. Those that have broken from the entrapment of racism are those that refuse to believe the narrative that they are inferior and are children of a lesser god. There is one God, one human race. You are part of that one human race that was created by God in His image. Who are you going to believe? May I submit that you believe what God says about you, not some social construct concocted by people driven by fear, hate, and ignorance?

All things work together for our good

Here is one of the most powerful scriptures that anybody in adversity should draw inspiration from because the life of Joseph clearly demonstrates that this is true. Paul, the apostle, writing to the church in Rome, said the following:

> *And we know that all things work together for good to those who love God, to those who are the called according to His purpose. Romans 8:28 (NKJV)*

Anybody looking at Joseph while he was still a slave and imprisoned would have ruled him out because his circumstances did not seem to align with the dream that he had for his life. He was deprived of physical freedom, and there was no way, humanly speaking, that he would become the leader his dreams had predicted. But God was with him and was working out everything for his good.

I point to God throughout the book because without God, our lives will not have the eternal impact that He intended them to have. To truly understand what is going on in our lives, community, and the world, we must factor God in the equation. Those who have decided to reject God have come up with some worldly solutions that have failed to deliver the peace, joy, contentment, purpose, and happiness that we all crave. Many have questioned why a good God will allow suffering, death, discrimination, hate, murder, and all the ills that we suffer from. There are many excellent resources that handle this subject better than I can, and you can refer to those. It is important to note that the life of Joseph demonstrates a simple truth that God will make use of the good, the bad, and the ugly because all things mean all things. Are you willing to trust God to make the most of whatever situation you are in? You can choose life, victory, hope, and happiness by trusting God to work all things for your good.

The 3 Hebrew boys and Daniel

While Joseph was sold by his brothers into slavery, three Hebrew boys Shadrach, Meshach, and Abednego together with Daniel were forcefully carried into exile from Judah by the Babylonians. How could God allow such a terrible thing to happen? Well, the people had sinned, and this was a punishment for their sin.

When these Hebrew boys were carried to Babylon, they did not allow bitterness, anger, and resentment to prevent them from working with God. They chose to obey God under this new reality of becoming servants to a pagan king. They could have easily allowed their circumstances to cause them to reject God and fit into their new environment, but they, just like Joseph, refused to defile themselves with the King's choice foods. Can you imagine the audacity of these boys refusing to eat what was presented to them by the King of Babylon? They were able to refuse to eat this food because they understood that God was the ultimate person in charge, and they had to obey him.

I mentioned these four Hebrew boys because even in captivity, they rose to prominence because they walked with God, obeyed his laws, and made use of their gifts. Because they identified problems and provided solutions, they were promoted to positions of leadership.

Daniel, for example, was so good with dreams that he could tell the dream and interpret it. We know this because King Nebuchadnezzar had a dream one night that troubled him so much that he woke up the next day and called his wise men to help him with the interpretation. The catch was that the person to interpret the dream had to start by telling him what the dream was.

> *The Chaldeans answered the king, and said, "There is not a man on earth who can tell the king's matter; therefore no king, lord, or ruler has ever asked such things of any magician, astrologer, or Chaldean. It is a difficult thing that the king requests, and there is no other who can tell it to the king except the gods, whose dwelling is not with flesh." Daniel 2:10-11 (NKJV)*

This was an impossible task, and the wise men told the king that only the gods could perform such a task, and it was not possible because the gods did not live among them. Here, you have the wise people of the land unable to solve a problem, and the king is getting agitated. He was not going to take no for an answer and proceeded to issue the following decree that sealed their fate:

> *For this reason the king was angry and very furious, and gave the command to destroy all the wise men of Babylon. So the decree went out, and they began killing the wise men; and they sought Daniel and his companions to kill them. Daniel 2:12-13 (NKJV)*

King Nebuchadnezzar was not somebody to joke with, and he wasted no time calling for the elimination of these people who claimed to know everything about dreams. This was when Daniel was called to save the day. Again, we see the power of knowing your gift and providing solutions. Daniel was not a Babylonian, but he served God and this made all the difference. He did not allow the fact that he was in captivity to prevent him from using his gift to serve his captor. This way of doing things does not fit with the narrative of vengeance, hate, anger, and bitterness. If Daniel had these heart issues, it would have prevented him from rising up to the occasion. He saved the day by telling the king his dream and the interpretation. The king rewarded him as follows:

> *Then the king promoted Daniel and gave him many great gifts; and he made him ruler over the whole province of Babylon, and chief administrator over all the wise men of Babylon. Also Daniel petitioned the king, and he set Shadrach, Meshach, and Abed-Nego over the affairs of the province of Babylon; but Daniel sat in the gate of the king. Daniel 2:48-49 (NKJV)*

When individuals identify and use their gifts, they rise up to the top. Unfortunately, many have decided to use skin pigmentation to determine who gets to the top because some believe that the color of their skin can hold them back. Daniel could have allowed the fact that he was not a Babylonian and a captive to prevent him from rising to the top, but he understood the power of using his gift because that is what matters the most.

As we draw the curtain on this chapter, it is important to understand that no matter where you are, what you have been through, and what other people have done to you, God can still make a way for you. Light can't be defeated by darkness, and it is not a good idea to fight darkness with darkness because it just does not work. While our natural tendency maybe to seek for vengeance and allow hate, bitterness, and resentment to lead us, we must resist this temptation. Like Joseph, we have to see the hand of God working in all circumstances for us.

Chapter 5:
The Way Forward

If a man like Malcolm X could change and repudiate racism, if I myself and other former Muslims can change, if young whites can change, then there is hope for America. Eldridge Cleaver

Not too long ago, I wrote something on Facebook about racism, and one of my contacts who happens to be African-American told me outright that I was not born here and I do not understand anything about racism. This person is not the only one who has told me that. I have not yet earned the right to speak on this issue because I do not understand it. We are one human family, and it will be unfair for me to write a book about such a sensitive issue like this without mentioning the African-American situation. After all, it is not me, but Martin Luther King, Jr. who said,

"I have a dream that my four little children will one day live in a nation where they will not be judged by the color of their skin but by the content of their character. I have a dream that one day every valley shall be exalted, and every hill and mountain shall be made low, the rough places will be made plain, and the crooked places will be made straight; "and the glory of the Lord shall be revealed, and all flesh shall see it together."[14]

As a little boy growing up in Africa, learning about the transatlantic and trans-Sahara slave trade and the horrors that our people were subjected to, it did not occur to me that I will one day write about these

---

[14] https://www.americanrhetoric.com/speeches/mlkihaveadream.htm

issues. In middle and high school, we studied about Martin Luther King, Jr. and the civil rights movement; little did I know that I will migrate to the United States of America and become part of the country.

The day I gave up my Cameroonian citizenship and embraced the United States of America as my new country, I also embraced her history with the good, the bad, and the ugly sides, and I care enough to bring solutions to the table. If I do not add my own perspective as somebody who is looking at what is going on in the country from a uniquely different perspective, I will be letting down my new country, and it will be extremely unfortunate if I did that. I am here for a time such as this, and just like Joseph in Egypt, he did not hold back when the country was facing a serious problem. He proposed a solution.

All I am doing here is presenting a solution that I think will move the country forward. The word of God is our only hope, and it will deliver what we need as a country and the world at large to navigate through this darkness that is threatening to engulf all of us. I, too, have a lot at stake because I am an American now and raising children in this country. When thinking about the type of country I want my children and grandchildren and great-grandchildren to be raised in, I think of the day when we will drop skin color as a basis of classifying and identifying each other. I dream of a day when there are no more hyphenated Americans, just "Americans" because that is who we are. I have told many people whenever I have the chance that we do not talk to each other enough and we are allowing ignorance to divide us. This is my attempt to initiate that conversation. You may not agree with everything I have said here but, at least, keep an open mind and let us have a dialogue.

There are too many parallels between the life of Joseph and the African-Americans in the United States of America. I am not speaking about their behavior because I am not wearing their shoes, but I am speaking the word of God here because many of them are people of the book. Thousands of books have been written on this issue and many solutions have been presented, and it is not possible to solve this complicated problem in a few paragraphs. That said, I have lived in the United States of America for more than 17 years and have interacted with people from different backgrounds. This may not be enough time to present a solution, but Joseph was in Egypt for less time. With the right attitude, he made a huge difference in the country. I am making an appeal to all who read this section to do so slowly and thoughtfully. There is a spiritual dimension that must be incorporated if anybody wants to make sense of what we are dealing with here.

Like Joseph, their brethren in Africa caught them and sold to Europeans. Those who were caught and sold did not deserve to be treated like this. Nothing can explain away the fact that hate, anger, and bitterness pushed Africans to catch their own brothers and sell them to foreigners without remorse. While some have argued that those who were sold into slavery were criminals and rejects of society, this justification is not enough. What crime did millions of people commit? Even if they committed a crime, the penalty was too severe. Another excuse that is given is that the Europeans lied to the Africans. Therefore, the Africans were not aware of the hellish conditions to which these slaves were going to be subjected. However, it makes no sense that a foreigner shows up and corrupts you with material stuff and you end up selling your own flesh and blood to them.

In the case of Joseph, his brothers thought that he was worth just 20 pieces of silver. Can you imagine his brothers thinking that his worth could be reduced to some arbitrary monetary value? Life is sacred and should never be reduced to the level of a commodity. Unfortunately, those on the African continent fell into this temptation because they thought gun powder, guns, gin, and other material things brought by the Europeans were worth more than their own flesh and blood. As you can clearly see here, they were not deceived, but the issues of the heart gravitated towards these material things. They allowed the hate, greed, and selfishness already in their hearts to take over, just as the Europeans and Arabs buying slaves and, at times, forcefully abducting some were driven by these same issues of the heart.

The brothers of Joseph were no different and they cannot justify their action under the pretext that their brother had shared his dreams that provoked them to sell him off. Cain did not kill Abel because he did something wrong. He committed the first murder out of anger and jealousy. He allowed his negative feelings towards the success of his brother to take over him, and he did the unthinkable. There was no racism here. Every time we try to pin racism on people who are allowing their sinful nature to rule over them, we are missing the point.

The Africans, like the brothers of Joseph, saw foreigners and sold their own flesh and blood without a second thought. Just like Joseph, these Africans were carried off to foreign lands under despicable conditions. Some of these slaves were resold to slave masters, just like Joseph.

They were not only enslaved but forced to build a lot of wealth for their slave masters. Joseph properly managing the business of his master Potiphar and made lots of money for him, and he did this without pay. The African-Americans were murdered, lunched, raped, exploited, and many terrible things were done to them. There is not enough room here to list all the atrocities that were committed against them. Some of the things were too despicable to mention. Joseph, too, was accused falsely and thrown in prison, not because of anything wrong that he did. He obeyed God by refusing to commit adultery, instead of being freed from slavery, he was thrown in prison for not sinning and going with the flow. It seemed God had abandoned him.

The life of Jesus Christ

Where was God when Joseph needed him the most? Where was God when the Africans caught their own brothers and sold them to foreigners? Where was God when all the despicable things were being done to the African slaves in the new world? How could God allow such wickedness to go unchecked? How could a loving, merciful, and good God allow such evil to be perpetuated?

I do not have any answers to these questions other than to say that it seems God must have been where he was when his own son Jesus Christ was being tortured, mocked, and brutalized by Roman soldiers. Jesus Christ had not committed a single crime, yet he was tried and condemned for no reason whatsoever.

When I was a little kid, I had a hard time understanding the meaning of Good Friday. How can the untimely death of a 33-year-old man on a bloody Roman cross be a "good" thing? How can death be good? How can defeat be a good thing? What good can come out of false accusations, jealousy, and hatred? These and many other questions plagued me as a kid. Good Friday cannot be good!

The unjust condemnation of an innocent man was handed down by one of the greatest "kangaroo courts" on the face of the earth based on trumped-up charges by zealous men with wicked intent for selfish gain.

The man under trial was betrayed by one of his close confidants who sold him for money. After spending three-and-a-half years with his master and teacher, he knew where to go get him. This confidant was entrusted with the "treasures", and he betrayed his master for 30 pieces of silver.

He led the soldiers, the chiefs, and the elders to the garden of Gethsemane. There, he identified his master by giving him a kiss. Yes! The kiss of betrayal which eventually led to the crucifixion of his master on a wooden cross by Roman soldiers.

During the trial, the accused man had no lawyer and no defense. Charges were levied against Him from all sides. Some people slapped him on the face and others spat on him. He was mocked, taunted, humiliated, and whipped in the public square for no reason.

During this whole ordeal, He did not struggle to defend himself, although He could. He did not try to free himself, although he could. After all, was He not a miracle worker? Had He not turned bread into wine, fed 5,000 people with 5 loaves of bread and 2 fishes? Was He not the one that raised the dead back to life?

His only chance of being freed was squashed by the very public that had benefited from all His good deeds. The people He healed, fed, delivered, encouraged, and comforted rejected Him. The people preferred a thief and murderer (Barabbas) to an innocent man and asked for the guilty one to be released instead of the innocent one. They shouted, "Crucify him, crucify him!" when asked if the innocent man should be released. The crowd was so worked up and agitated and demanded the blood of an innocent man.

Pilate, the Roman governor, had the power to set this innocent man free but chose not to because of political correctness and the desire to protect his job.

He washed his hands and failed to take responsibility for his actions. How can this be? How can such injustice be done so callously?

You will be surprised by what people will do when it comes to advancing their own agenda, when it comes to climbing the corporate ladder, winning an election, getting promotion and a raise.

The condemned man was made to carry His own cross to the place where He was going to be crucified. When He arrived at the place of his death, two other condemned thieves were there already.

The Roman soldiers stripped Him naked and nailed him on a wooden cross. He died a shameful, disgraceful, painful and disgusting death among two convicted criminals. How can this be a good thing? It was a bloody mess, to say the least.

You will be surprised to hear that His only "crime" is LOVE. This 33-year-old man loved others more than His own life. In His own words, He said,

"There is no greater love than to lay down one's life for one's friends. For even the Son of Man came not to be served but to serve others and to give his life as a ransom for many."

Love is more than feelings and emotions. Love requires sacrifice and in His case, death.

Perhaps, you are wondering what this has to do with you, or where you fit in. The life of this innocent 33-year-old man who was brutally killed has influenced my own life profoundly, and I think there is much we can learn from Him.

Jesus of Nazareth, the man I was talking about, was on a mission and stayed on course. He did not give up and did not quit, even when the going got extremely difficult, unpopular, and dangerous.

It got to the point where He laid down His own life willfully because He was a man of principle. Paul says this about him, *"Being found in appearance as a man, He humbled Himself by becoming obedient to the point of death, even death on a cross."*

His obedience cost him His life. He could have taken the road of least resistance. He could have done what was politically correct. He could have done what was popular and acceptable to many.

Yet, He challenged the status quo and the establishment. He took the road less traveled. He chose death over life. He died so that others will live.

Many people ask why a good and benevolent God allows so much suffering in the world. Before you give up on God, remember that Jesus of Nazareth was both man and God and he suffered and died a bloody death on the cross.

Have you been betrayed? Jesus and Joseph were, and the Africans who were sold into slavery!

Have you been unjustly treated? Jesus and Joseph were, and the Africans who were sold into slavery!

Have you been rejected? Jesus and Joseph were, and the Africans who were sold into slavery!

Have you been wrongfully convicted? Jesus and Joseph were, and the Africans who were sold into slavery!

Have you been abandoned and forsaken by those you love and trust? Jesus and Joseph were, and the Africans who were sold into slavery!

Have you been ridiculed, misunderstood and mischaracterized? Jesus and Joseph were, and the Africans who were sold into slavery!

Have you been shamed, wrongfully accused? Jesus and Joseph were, and the Africans who were sold into slavery!

Have you been sold by those you trusted? Jesus and Joseph were, and the Africans who were sold into slavery!

Are you under tremendous pressure to quit? Jesus and Joseph were, and the Africans who were sold into slavery!

Are you weary and tired? Jesus and Joseph were, and the Africans who were sold into slavery!

What made Jesus and Joseph succeed and what will make you succeed is making up your mind never to give up no matter what! Never quit no matter what! Above all, it is seeing and accepting God's involvement in the whole process. God uses the good, the bad, and the ugly to accomplish his purpose when we surrender everything to him.

Jesus died and out of His death came the forgiveness of our sins and billions all over the world have found peace, life, and hope in Him.

Make your life count by walking in love and treating others how you want to be treated. Good Friday is indeed good because the untimely, brutal, and unjust death of a 33-year-old man has reconciled us to God.

God always has the last say, and it is our responsibility to trust Him to make all wrongs right. In the case of Jesus Christ, those who killed

Him under the influence of the devil did not know that they were facilitating the provision of salvation and redemption for all mankind.

This is why Jesus, while He was hanging on the bloody Roman cross under intense pain and anguish, did not curse or call for social justice. Instead, Jesus said,

Then Jesus said, "Father, forgive them, for they do not know what they do." Luke 23:34 (NKJV)

Instead of asking for his tormentors and killers to be killed, Jesus asked for their forgiveness because He understood the bigger plan of God for his life and He knew who was actually in charge.

You may say that Jesus was able to forgive because He was God in the flesh and understood the beginning from the end. What about Joseph? How did he handle the betrayal from his brothers? Did he call the wrath of God on them, or ask for them to be punished? Even though Joseph had the power to order the execution of his brothers, he forgave them because he understood that God was in control and had the final say.

Forgiveness is for the strong, not the weak. Choosing to forgive does not mean that you are saying that atrocities were not committed or that the atrocities were not painful. You forgive because anger, bitterness, and resentment will eventually eat you up and prevent you from benefiting from what God has in mind for you.

Therefore, the way forward is to seek enlightenment, to see the bigger picture of what God is up to because He is aware of all the betrayals and atrocities that were committed against the Africans that were forcefully uprooted from African soil and brought to the New World. There are many descendants of these Africans living in the Caribbean, South American, and the United States of America. When they look at what transpired to be where they are right now, it is not good, but based on God's word, it is going to be more profitable to let God be God in the situation and forgive. This is not a popular message or a comfortable one, but the alternative is worse. It is better to trust God than your feelings. There is a lot of anger, bitterness, and resentment, but it will only destroy you if not neutralized by love and forgiveness. This message is for those who are people of the book. You must lead the way and teach other people to do the same. There are those who have been advocating for vengeance and payback, but this approach is not helpful because it does not work.

When you forgive, it frees you from your enemy. While it may not feel natural, but it is possible because we have the capacity to forgive.

Racism cannot stand forgiveness because they are incompatible. Now is the time to drive out darkness by letting the light of God that is in you to shine. Do not allow political correctness or the calls for payback that some are advocating to cover your light. God never left you because nothing can separate us from the love of God that is in Christ Jesus.

Ask God to open your eyes to see the bigger picture and what He is up to because God is always up to something. Joseph did not suffer in vain, and the suffering of Jesus Christ was not wasted either. Your own suffering and that of your people will not be wasted if you let God be God!

Now is the right time to rise up and begin to provide solutions and in so doing, you will rise up to the top. You have special gifts and you should start deploying them because the United States of America has a lot of problems that need solutions.

Chapter 6:
The End of Racism

I refuse to accept the view that mankind is so tragically bound to the starless midnight of racism and war that the bright daybreak of peace and brotherhood can never become a reality... I believe that unarmed truth and unconditional love will have the final word. Martin Luther King, Jr.

The title of this chapter is a paradox because throughout the book, I pointed out that racism is a social construct, a façade, a bogeyman that has morphed into a monster that is extremely difficult to define and contain. Yet, here I am talking about its end. The idea of racism is entrenched in my heart and it is in the news every day. It has been said that "If you tell a lie to people repeatedly, it will be accepted as the truth." We have been bombarded with the idea of racism to the extent it is almost heresy to dare suggest that it is just a social construct. There are people who strongly believe that racism is real and very tangible, and they see everything through the eyes of race. They have been so brainwashed into thinking that people are divided by the color of their skin. It is absurd that the white and black classification permeates every segment of our society. I mentioned that in Bamumbu, white people are referred to as red. Therefore, we will have a red and black division, an indication that using color to classify people does not make sense.

The intention of this book was not to dwell on the negativity associated with racism, ethnocentrism, and tribalism. Care was taken to demonstrate that a social construct such as racism has no place in any civilized society, but it has persisted because society continues to give life to it. In this final chapter of the book, I am going to hammer the last nail on the coffin in which racism is to be placed and bury it.

The call in this book is for individual action because society is made up of individuals. When each person begins to change, other people will follow. As we bury racism, you will realize that some people will not do it because it is a personal choice. I want you to no longer be at the mercy of any social construct, and I want you to break free from any unfounded opinions about you. I want you to know who you are, affirm it, and walk in that realization. Trying to change the ignorant and bigoted person is not your job. While we hope those who believe that they are superior will change, you have to move on with just changing yourself because only you can change yourself. While you may fail to change others, your chances of changing yourself are much higher.

Here are some of the things that will put an end to racism, once and for all. All of these are going to be focusing on what you can do to change you. If your focus is changing other people, you are going to get frustrated, discouraged, and will give up.

1. Know who you are

When you know who you truly are, nobody is going to mess with your mind. I have shown that racism is a social construct based on a faulty ideology about people's identity. According to the racist, there are some people whose skin color makes them inferior to them and deserve to be treated as such. However, it is not enough for somebody to believe that your skin color or any other thing makes you inferior to them. To be inferior, you need to believe that you are inferior. As simple as this may sound, many have stumbled over this basic and foundational idea that all are created equal because some have a hard time believing that they are not superior and others cannot shake off the idea that they are not *inferior.*

Knowing who you is the best place to start because if you do not know who you are, you are going to behave contrary to who you truly are. Take, for example, a prince who is born to a royal family but was taken to a farmer to be raised as a farmer will think, talk and act as a farmer because that is all he knows. If he is taken back to the place and convinced that he is indeed a prince, his actions will change and he will start carrying himself as the royalty that he rightfully is.

You are not the result of a cosmic accident because you have been created in the image of God. God Himself has declared that we are all created in His image. We are all the same.

If you think the issue of knowing your identity is something that is not crucial, you have to consider the fact that the devil himself attacked Jesus Christ in this very area. Jesus had been fasting in the desert for 40 days and was hungry. Then, the devil showed up:

Now when the tempter came to Him, he said, "If You are the Son of God, command that these stones become bread."

But He answered and said, "It is written, 'Man shall not live by bread alone, but by every word that proceeds from the mouth of God.' " Matthew 4:3-4 (NKJV)

Take a close look at the sneaky attempt of the devil to try and make Jesus Christ doubt who He truly was. The devil understood that if he could make Jesus Christ doubt who He was, He would start acting in ways that are contrary to who He was. What somebody believes about themselves determines their actions. Do you think that the devil doubted who Jesus Christ was? Yet, he dared Jesus to affirm or reject that fact that He was indeed the Son of God.

Jesus was hungry after 40 days of fasting in the wilderness, and the devil tried to tie His legitimate need for food to His identity. Today, many have fallen into this trap of tying their identity to their sexual needs and any other needs that they have. Can you imagine how Jesus felt after He had not eaten for 40 days? He was hungry, but He refused to give the devil a foothold by doubting who He was. Jesus did not waste time arguing with the devil and did not try to prove to him that He was the Son of God. Instead, He quoted the word of God.

You have to know who you are and believe what the word of God says about you. When people want you to doubt your true identity in Christ, you should use the sword of the spirit, which is the word of God. You do not need to prove to these people that you are not a cosmic accident and no chimpanzee's cousin or monkey's uncle. You are who God, your Creator, says you are —and that is good enough.

The devil was not done with Jesus and attacked His identity a second time. I bring this up because the enemy is relentless in trying to make you doubt who you are and believe a lie.

It is amazing that the devil knows the word of God and can quote it, but he was trying to misinterpret the word of God here by asking Jesus to put up a public stunt.

Then the devil took Him up into the holy city, set Him on the pinnacle of the temple, and said to Him, "If You are the Son of God, throw Yourself down. For it is written:

'He shall give His angels charge over you,'

And,

'In their hands they shall bear you up,

Lest you dash your foot against a stone.'"

Jesus said to him, "It is written again, 'You shall not tempt the Lord your God.'" Matthew 4:5-7 (NKJV)

Can you imagine how many people would have believed Jesus if He jumped from the top of the temple and landed on the ground without any harm? This would have been an excellent publicity stunt and would have benefited His mission of reconciling people back to God tremendously. But Jesus knew better; He knew that He had to die on the cross for His mission to be accomplished. He was not going to take a shortcut and put up a show for the public.

Your identity is who God says you are, not what any government, textbook, or group of experts say. Just because man-made laws say you are something, it does not make it true. Therefore, it is important to keep believing and affirming who you truly are.

2. You are a child of God

In addition to being created in the image and likeness of God, you become a child of God when you recognize that the fellowship between you and God needs to be reestablished. You become born of God when you believe in the name of Jesus Christ. For it is written:

But as many as received Him, to them He gave the right to become children of God, to those who believe in His name: who were born, not of blood, nor of the will of the flesh, nor of the will of man, but of God. John 1:12-13 (NKJV)

For as many as are led by the Spirit of God, these are sons of God. For you did not receive the spirit of bondage again to fear, but you received the Spirit of adoption by whom we cry out, "Abba, Father." The Spirit Himself bears witness with our spirit that we are children of God, and if children, then heirs—heirs of God and joint heirs with Christ, if indeed we suffer from Him, that we may also be glorified together. Romans 8: 14-17 (NKJV)

When you become a child of God, you receive the Spirit of God and become a joint heir with Jesus Christ. There is nothing more powerful than understanding this new reality that you are a child of God. Do not let anybody tell you otherwise. With God on your side, you are the majority and you are unstoppable.

3. You are not inferior

Since we have already established that you are a child of God, it automatically means that you are not inferior. Do not let what others think about you to become your reality. Some may have even said that you are inferior to them and cannot amount to anything. You have to reject such pronouncements and believe who God says you are. To act contrary to this will be detrimental to your well-being, and it will keep you trapped in the grip of racism.

Some may want you to believe that you are the child of a lesser god, you are not because if you believe in God Almighty, you are His child, just as any other person who believes.

Some people think that they are better than others and even act on these thoughts and discriminate against other people. They are living in self-delusion. There is one race—the human race— and we are all equal, although not the same. It is unfortunate that physical features such as the pigmentation of one's skin, the color of their hair and shape of their nose are used to define who they are. People who subscribe to this type of thinking do not have their facts straight. They are wrong and will always be wrong. Therefore, do not listen to them!

Racism is driven by fear, ignorance, greed, and selfishness. There is no scientific evidence for the subdivision of the human race, so all these divisions are social constructs that have no empirical basis. Sadly, many people are allowing the ignorance of other people to influence how they view themselves and what they believe about themselves. Let God be right and let any other person be wrong. It is written you are fearfully and wonderfully made, you are the apple of God's eye, and you are created in His image and likeness. If you believe this, then racism will bow at your feet.

It is important for you to note that what you believe about yourself is what people sense when they meet you.

Therefore, instead of trying to change the racist, focus on changing your belief system. For racism to work, it needs two kinds of people: those who, out of ignorance, believe and act as if they are superior and those who believe that they are inferior because they have been told they are. You may be saying right now that racism goes beyond what happens between two individuals, that it is institutionalized. This is where laws must be passed to counteract institutionalized racism. That is why, in some countries, good laws have been passed to fight racism and discrimination, but the laws alone will not deliver.

The laws are ineffective because racism is a malady of the heart, it needs internal transformation, not external legislation. The old belief system of superiority must be replaced by the basic fact that there is only one human race, and no one is more human than the other. The next step of the process is a change in the belief system of the people who have been conditioned to believe that they are inferior.

Inferiority complex is a malady of the heart as well, and laws can only do so much to liberate people from this phantom. Many lives have been destroyed, and so much potential lost because of wrong programming. After the persistent and constant bombardment of derogatory messages and fabricated lies, people internalize these lies and start believing them.

What you believe is what you are eventually going to act on. The truth is simple: none of us was consulted to be born on a particular continent, and we had nothing to do with the color of our skin, hair, and shape of our nose. Therefore, there is no point in wishing to be somebody else. Your mission in life is tied to the tools and resources you were born with. Now is the time to start appreciating and leveraging those things that are unique and particular about you.

The worst trap is that of having a victim mentality and playing the blame game. "They did this to me. They said this about me. They treated me like this. They think about me like this." What do YOU believe about yourself? How do YOU treat yourself? What do YOU tell yourself?

There is never any justification for hatred or any other racist tendencies, and these behaviors should and must always be condemned. That said, no matter what somebody says to you or how they act towards you and treat you, it is your reaction that determines the outcome. You relinquish your power when you allow the victim mentality and blame game to take hold of you.

Focus on developing mental toughness and strengthening your belief system. This approach will deliver you from mental slavery and break the invisible shackles that racism is trying to bind you with.

4. Nothing can separate you from the love of God

This is a truth that you have to anchor your life on because racism cannot stand against this truth. You are loved by God, and nothing will be able to separate you from His love. Nothing means nothing. You should bear in mind that racism thrives when we keep the love of God out of the picture and feel that we are at the mercy of other people. From this point forward, take the following scriptures to heart:

> *What then shall we say to these things? If God is for us, who can be against us? He who did not spare His own Son, but delivered Him up for us all, how shall He not with Him also freely give us all things? Who shall bring a charge against God's elect? It is God who justifies. Who is he who condemns? It is Christ who died, and furthermore is also risen, who is even at the right hand of God, who also makes intercession for us. Who shall separate us from the love of Christ? Shall tribulation, or distress, or persecution, or famine, or nakedness, or peril, or sword? Romans 8:31-35 (NKJV)*

God has already offered His only Son for the redemption of our sins, and there is nothing more important than His Son. The promise is clear: God will give us all other things. I pray that you draw some comfort from these verses as you stand in your position in Christ and pronounce who you are.

If you still doubt what nothing really means, you should consider the fact that you have already been promised victory in Christ. Paul, the apostle, ensured that he listed some of the things that people may easily think will separate them from God:

Yet in all these things we are more than conquerors through Him who loved us. For I am persuaded that neither death nor life, nor angels nor principalities nor powers, nor things present nor things to come, nor height nor depth, nor any other created thing, shall be able to separate us from the love of God which is in Christ Jesus our Lord. Romans 8:37-39 (NKJV)

There is nothing more important than knowing that you are loved by God. This is a secure place to be and from there, you will be able to defeat racism and any other thing that may be brought against you. There is no need to despair because you are not on your own. God is on your side and will see you through. He has promised to love you no matter what. All you need to do is to trust Him.

5. Racism and Christianity do not mix

There is no way this book will end without touching on this sensitive issue because there are some who say they have been put off because the church is racist. *Racism and Christianity should not appear in the same sentence. There has been a history of segregation in the Christian church and this must not be condoned.* We are supposed to be the children of the light to show the world how to treat all God's children.

Unfortunately, we are living in a fallen world. Some of us who are supposed to be mature are still babies in the faith and are drinking milk instead of eating solid food. Are all people created in the image and likeness of God? Do we pay lip service to this and in our hearts believe and expect the contrary? What makes anybody think they are superior to others? What makes anybody believe they are inferior? It takes the person who believes they are superior and the one who believes they are inferior for this toxic virus of racism to spread. This toxic virus is fueled by fear. The Scripture declares that we have not been given a spirit of fear. Can the church stand up and be light and salt, instead of a country club?

I know I have asked too many questions and will not answer them because we should not be asking these questions in the first place. If you have read the book carefully, you must have the answers by now. Nobody in the body of Christ should feel that they are superior or inferior. We are all one in Christ, and this is not a suggestion, it is a fact. Anything else is not sanctioned by Scripture.

Unfortunately, some of the Christians have allowed fear and societal pressure to tell them how to relate to other people. This is not correct because our marching orders are from God and are spelled out in Scripture. If we insist on doing our own thing and forming churches that do not reflect the diversity in our communities, then we are setting up country clubs, not churches. The church is the body of Christ, and if your community has people from different ethnic groups, the churches in that community must reflect this reality.

Some people say this is a difficult thing to do because people are more comfortable with their own kind and they like to do what comes naturally to them. Humanly speaking, this makes a lot of sense, but we are the people of God and have not been called to do what comes naturally to us. We are called to be the hands, feet, and eyes of Christ and to carry our cross and follow Jesus Christ daily. I had already touched on this issue of being called to carry our cross daily in one of the previous chapters, and it is being restated here because the idea of being comfortable permeates our society today and has invaded the church.

We should not be afraid to belong to the same church with people from different ethnic backgrounds just because we are afraid that our children may intermarry and we will lose our social status. There is more to following Jesus Christ than maintaining our cultures and social status. Jesus did not die for us to preserve our culture.

Many people claim they are not racist, but their thoughts and actions betray them. When you hear their private conversations about other ethnic groups, you will be shocked. These same people do not have friends from different ethnic groups because they do not trust people who do not look like them.

I am not only writing to the Christians in the west. This is for Christians all over the globe. I mentioned what the popular Kenyan law professor and advocate for the eradication of corruption on Africa said, *"The blood of ethnicity among the African Christians is stronger than the blood of Christ."*

This is a very sad reality that must change. The church can and must do better because the world is looking up to us to lead the way. Now is the time to tear down the barriers that we have set up and open the church up to other people. We need to learn about other people, visit them, invite them over to have meals on our tables. While it is great to meet in the church building, it is greater to meet at home over a meal and listen to each other.

You cannot practice Christianity and racism at the same time. If you think this is possible, you are still in your spiritual diapers, and it is time for you to grow up. We are one in Christ and should act as such.

6. You have the final say

The ball is in your court! You have the power to kick it towards any direction you choose. This book is about you as an individual, not about the government, institution or organization. I mentioned that the governments, laws, and organizations are the other players in this issue, but the main thrust of this book has been YOU. There is no point in chasing the wind because you will never be able to catch it. I say this to underscore the important fact that you should stop focusing on those that believe to be superior because they are not. Stop believing those who believe that you are inferior and treat you as if you are.

The power is in your hands because when you refuse to believe what other people say about you, it will render it useless.

This book is not only for those that feel that they are inferior; it is for those that believe that they are superior. It may be shocking to hear that you are not superior, but whoever told you that you are superior to others lied to your face. It is time for you to come down from your high horse and face the reality that "All men are created in the image of God." Therefore, you should stop being part of the problem and start being the solution by treating all people with respect, honor, and dignity. You are not going to lose anything if you treat other people right. When everybody is empowered to reach their full potential, you, too, will benefit.

Stop using skin color to classify and treat people. There is, has been, and always will be one human race. This may be a hard truth to swallow, but it is the truth that will set both the oppressed and the oppressor free. Anybody that accepts this truth, believes, and acts on it can boldly and confidently ask, "Racism, where is thy sting?" The good news is that there is no sting because we are all equally created in the image and likeness of God. There are no children of a lesser God!

Chapter 7:
The Banishment of
Racism Now and Forever

O death, where is thy sting? O grave, where is thy victory?
The sting of death is sin; and the strength of sin is the law.
But thanks be to God, which giveth us the victory through our Lord Jesus
Christ. 1 Corinthians 15:55-57

If I did not care about the eradication of racism, this book would not have been written. But racism is just the symptom of a much more devastating problem — SIN. The book started with the first murder in human history. This heinous act was motivated by jealousy and hate. When we traced the origin of such feelings, it took us back to the Garden of Eden. This is where the human heart became corrupt because Adam and Eve sinned. All of us are descendants of Adam and Eve. Therefore, by default, we have adopted this SIN nature from them. We are corrupt and this corruption manifests itself through racism and other vices.

In other words, we are born in sin and sin rules over us. Since racism is just the symptom of a bigger and much deeper problem, we have to dig deeper to solve it. All of us have a reference point from which we analyze whatever problem or challenge we are facing. Mine happened to be a Judeo-Christian perspective. This explains why in the course of writing the book, I draw a lot from the Bible to illustrate the origin of racism and how it can be defeated and banished forever.

I am not under any illusion that there is a magic wand that can be waved to make racism disappear. There is no silver bullet either. The fact that we are writing about this troubling topic is a testament to how difficult it has been to eradicate it. This does not mean that there is no hope though. The solutions I presented in this book to the best of my ability are based on the Judeo-Christian teachings that have been passed down to us over the years as revealed in Holy Scripture. I will be doing you a great disservice if I do not present the information here because, on your own, you will not be able to make it.

Since racism is a manifestation of SIN, it is more profitable to eradicate sin because when that is done, racism will automatically be eradicated. To deal with this fundamental problem of sin, I will be presenting what has worked for me for your consideration. All I ask of you is that you read through it and decide for yourself.

This book was written with the assumption that you are a born-again child of God. If you are not, this is an opportunity for you to learn how to become a child of God. The only way you can become a minister of reconciliation is by, first of all, being reconciled to God. It is impossible to give what you do not have or show other people the way you do not know. This entire chapter has been written to allow you to consider becoming connected to God, who is the source of all things.

Before we continue, permit me to say congratulations! You have done what many people do not. Most people start books and never finish reading them. You persevered, and now you are here. There is nothing more important than being a child of God. I will be wicked if I do not share this truth with you. It is one of the most important things that you will ever do. It is more important than taking care of your physical body because your body will eventually decay. While it is crucial for you not to damage your body by taking sugar, your body will eventually die. There is a part of you that is more important: your spirit that is eternal. Therefore, you must take care of your spirit.

I do not know where you are in your own spiritual journey. No matter where you are, I strongly encourage you to read this chapter, reflect on it, and make sure that you put things right with God. You are being offered an opportunity to have God come and live in you. This should excite you more than having the perfect body.

When our Lord Jesus Christ says something, we must take it seriously. Here is one of the most important Bible verses that puts everything in perspective:

For what profit is it to a man if he gains the whole world, and loses his own soul? Or what will a man give in exchange for his soul? Matthew 16:26 (NKJV)

Here Jesus Christ is asking a profound question that everybody must answer. You cannot afford to keep going through life without answering this question because how your life ends will determine the answer to these questions. Interestingly, the body is not mentioned in the verse. The soul is what is front and center because the body will finally die and decay, but the soul is going to live forever.

There is nothing more important than your soul, so you should take this seriously. While there is nothing wrong with being successful in this life, if you neglect what is more important, you are going to have all of eternity to regret it.

The major assumption that has been throughout this book is that you are a believer in the Lord Jesus Christ. This implies that you have given your life to Him and accepted Him as your Lord and Savior. In addition to being born again, you are walking daily with the Lord and bearing the fruit of the Holy Spirit.

Having an eternal perspective is the ultimate because, at the end of the day, it is eternal that matters. People have looked for the foundation of youth over the ages, and there is a lot of research right now to understand aging and how to reverse it. Even if we were to find the fountain of youth and drink from it so that we remain young forever, life on earth would still have a lot of changes for us. We are still going to face other many other challenges because we are living in a fallen world with many different problems.

I say all this to emphasize the importance of looking forward to our true and final home, where we will be with our Heavenly Father forever and ever. While life on earth is great, life in heaven is going to be greater and more fulfilling. This is something that all of God's children have to look forward to.

If you are not yet a child of God, here is your opportunity for you to learn how to become a child of God.

Instructions for eternal life

Life does not end when you die. There is an afterlife, and I am going to use this opportunity to tell you about it. Talking about the afterlife is not an indirect way for you to disengage with the present life, but a motivation for you to make the most of your time on earth. While there are many arguments about which road leads to God and which of God is true, I am not going to dwell on these issues. The reason being that there is not enough room for us to do a comparative study of world religions.

It is important to note that while popular culture classifies Christianity as a religion and tries to compare it with other religions, the truth is that it is not a religion. Religion is mankind trying their best to reach out to God and please him.

Christianity is the exact opposite because God is the person who is reaching out to mankind and doing all to redeem us. To enjoy this redemption that God is offering, you must follow instructions.

I am writing this with the assumption that you have been reconciled with God and have a relationship with Him. If you do not yet have a relationship with God, I am going to give you the opportunity here to take care of that. This is one of the most important decisions you will ever make and should not take it lightly. I do not want you to allow the failures of other believers that you might have interacted with to prevent you from getting into a personal relationship with your heavenly Father. He has been waiting for you to come home and be reunited with Him.

Here is your opportunity to come home to the fullness of abundant life. All that you need and desire is in God; you will never be forsaken or abandoned.

Let me start by asking you this: do you have a personal relationship with Jesus Christ? This question is being asked because although all roads lead to Rome, not all roads lead to the God of the Bible. Jesus Christ, who is God incarnate, made some exclusive claims when He said,

"Jesus answered, "I am the way and the truth and the life. No one comes to the Father except through me." John 14:6 (NIV)

This is a bold claim, and Jesus Christ died for standing up for this. He is simply saying that if you want a relationship with the God of the Bible, who is also the creator of heaven and earth, you must pass through Him. If you are not a yet a follower of Jesus Christ, here is your opportunity to do so. I suggest this because it is going to get you connected to the source of all things. You will become spiritually alive and will live forever in the presence of God. Raising your child with the fear of God is the best thing you can do for you and your child.

The first and most important thing to understand is that we have all sinned. In other words, we cannot meet God's perfect standard, no matter how hard we try. Have you tried on your own to be good and realized the many times you did not measure up? Do you struggle with a void in your heart that nothing has been able to fill, no matter how hard you tried? Are you comparing yourself to others and feeling that you are good because you are better than other people? If you answered yes to any these questions, you need to understand that all of us have sinned, just as the following scriptures clearly spell out:

"For all have sinned, and come short of the glory of God." (Romans 3:23)

"For there is not a just man upon earth, that doeth good, and sinneth not." (Ecclesiastes 7:20)

"But we are all as an unclean thing, and all our righteousnesses are as filthy rags, and we all do fade as a leaf; and our iniquities, like the wind, have taken us away." (Isaiah 64:6)

"As it is written, There is none righteous, no, not one:" (Romans 3:10)

"For whosoever shall keep the whole law, and yet offend in one point, he is guilty of all." (James 2:10)

"If we say that we have no sin, we deceive ourselves, and the truth is not in us." (1 John 1:8)

We have all sinned and need God's forgiveness. This is the place to start. When you acknowledge this, then you will be able to receive God's free forgiveness and salvation.

The third crucial thing to understand is the devastating consequences of sin.

You may be wondering why sin is such a bad thing and why I am making such a big deal about it. Everybody, including you, should be concerned about the consequences of sin:

For the wages of sin is death, but the free gift of God is eternal life in Christ Jesus, our Lord. Romans 6:23 ESV

Therefore, just as sin came into the world through one man, and death through sin, and so death spread to all men because all sinned. Romans 5:12 ESV

But as for the cowardly, the faithless, the detestable, as for murderers, the sexually immoral, sorcerers, idolaters, and all liars, their portion will be in the lake that burns with fire and sulfur, which is the second death. Revelation 21:8 ESV

This death is both physical and spiritual. Sin can cause us to die in this life, and if we die in sin, we will be separated from God forever. You do not want this to happen to you and your child or children. You want to be able to live forever in the presence of God. This is why it is crucial to think about the wages of sin.

The fourth crucial step is to ask God to forgive our sins. The good news is that God has already made provision for that and is ready and willing to forgive all our sins. God has already made the first move!

"For God so loved the world, that he gave his only begotten Son, that whosoever believeth in him should not perish, but have everlasting life."(John 3:16)

"Jesus said unto her, I am the resurrection, and the life: he that believeth in me, though he were dead, yet shall he live: And whosoever liveth and believeth in me shall never die. Believest thou this?" (John 11:25-26)

"And they said, Believe on the Lord Jesus Christ, and thou shalt be saved, and thy house." (Acts 16:31)

"That if thou shalt confess with thy mouth the Lord Jesus, and shalt believe in thine heart that God hath raised him from the dead, thou shalt be saved. {10} For with the heart man believeth unto righteousness; and with the mouth confession is made unto salvation." (Romans 10:9-10)

"Whosoever believeth that Jesus is the Christ is born of God: and every one that loveth him that begat loveth him also that is begotten of him." (1 John 5:1)

Now that you have confessed and asked Jesus to forgive your sins, your sins have been forgiven and will be remembered no more.

The fifth and final thing to do is invite Jesus into your heart. Now is your opportunity to surrender your life to Jesus. Jesus will never force himself on anyone. According to the following scripture, He is outside knocking and waiting for you to invite Him to come in:

Behold, I stand at the door, and knock: if any man hear my voice, and open the door, I will come in to him, and will sup with him, and he with me." (Revelation 3:20)

"But as many as received him, to them gave he power to become the sons of God, even to them that believe on his name:" (John 1:12)

"And because ye are sons, God hath sent forth the Spirit of his Son into your hearts, crying, Abba, Father." (Galatians 4:6)

"That Christ may dwell in your hearts by faith; that ye, being rooted and grounded in love," (Ephesians 3:17)

Jesus Christ is waiting for you to invite Him to come in and you can do that by praying and asking him to do so. Use your own words to talk to Him or use *"The Sinner's Prayer"* by John Barnett.

The following prayer expresses the desire to transfer trust to Christ alone for eternal salvation. If its words speak of your own heart's desire, praying them can be the link that will connect you to God.

Dear God, I know that I am a sinner, and there is nothing that I can do to save myself. I confess my complete helplessness to forgive my own sin or to work my way to heaven. At this moment, I trust Christ alone as the One who bore my sin when He died on the cross. I believe that He did all that will ever be necessary for me to stand in your holy presence. I thank you that Christ was raised from the dead as a guarantee of my own resurrection. As best as I can, I now transfer my trust to Him. I am grateful that He has promised to receive me despite my many sins and failures. Father, I take you at your word. I thank you that I can face death now that you are my Savior. Thank you for the assurance that you will walk with me through the deep valley. Thank you for hearing this prayer. In Jesus' name. Amen.

Praise God! Hallelujah! If you just said this prayer, I am super excited for you and want to use this opportunity to welcome you into the kingdom of God and God's family. This is one of the most important decisions you will ever make because it has eternal consequences. You are now a newborn baby in Christ and need spiritual nourishment to grow in your faith. If you need more information on what to do next, send me an email.

It is extremely important that you understand the crucial nature of this decision you have just made. I want to highlight the fact that the focus has not been for you to join a religion or to become religious. Religion is a man seeking to please God. Here, we have presented a picture of God seeking man. God loved the entire world, then gave His son to pay the penalty for our sins. This point is being made so that you understand that you are being called into a personal relationship with Jesus and not just some religious observances. While church membership is important, it is more important that you establish a strong and vibrant relationship with Jesus Christ.

Going forward with God

Our lives on earth pale in comparison to eternity. There is no comparison at all because eternity has no measure. If you live to be more than 100 years on earth, you will not make it to 200 years. This implies that no matter what you do, your life on this side has a limit. Therefore, the best thing to do is to factor in eternity in the equation of your life.

This is what you have just done, and I applaud you for that. Now that you have become a child of God, it is important for you to learn how to walk with Him. You need to learn how to love God and know Him.

When we love somebody, we spend time with them, talk to them and get to know them. This is not done in a day, but it takes time. You just started this relationship with your heavenly Father, and you have to learn how to know Him and grow in intimacy with Him. If you need resources on what to do, please contact me at eternalkingdom101@ gmail.com.

Acknowledgment

I want to thank my Heavenly Father for revealing Himself and the divine truths expressed in this book. Nothing transformed me more than the realization that I am a child of God, and that nothing can separate me from His love.

A special thanks to my parents Mr. Abraham Lekunze and Mrs. Celine Lekunze, who instilled the fear of God at a tender age and gave me the room to express myself. When it came to choosing my wife, they did not object to the choice I made.

Without the support and encouragement of my wife Elizabeth Tayem, this book would not have been possible. She is my #1 fan, critic, support, and encourager. Above all, she accepted to embark on this journey with me. We have learned a lot, and there is still a lot to learn. She has allowed me to live the message in this book, and I will forever be grateful.

Our children have had to put up with the long hours spent behind the keyboard as I typed this book. It took longer than it should have because I am still working on my typing speed. Our children Afaamba, Ntsomboma, Elotmboma, Abeutmboma, and Atseamboma remind me of our uniqueness and special qualities. Although they are all born by us, they are unique and gifted differently.

Many people have demonstrated that the message in this book is practical and applicable. Dr. Erel Little has been a friend for more than 16 years since we moved to the United States, and we have been through a lot together. He embraced us even though he is Caucasian. He has been so understanding. We have shared countless meals and moments together, and that has made a lot of difference in our lives.

Special thanks to Dr. James Carter who is not only my mentor, teacher, and graduate advisor, he has become a dear friend. He has demonstrated that we have so much in common and very little that should divide us. We have fellowshipped together, and my kids consider him as their grandpa.

Another person that has been a good friend and with whom we have lived life together is Raeline Marie. She is the one that has demonstrated servant leadership and appreciated what we are doing for the United States of America.

I also would like to thank all the students that fellowshipped with us in our apartment while we were graduate students at the University of Texas at Dallas. We had students from all ethnicities, and they, too, demonstrated that we can get along. In Christ, we are all one.

My editors deserve a special thanks because their diligence and hard work turned my ramblings into a cohesive book that you have enjoyed reading. Without their input, this book would not have been possible.

The design team of **IEM PRESS** did a fantastic job in getting this book ready for my readers. I do not know what I would have done without them.

About the Author

D r. Eric Tangumonkem was born and raised in a Caldera on the Cameroon Volcanic Line in Cameroon West Africa. He has a Bachelor's degree in Geology and a minor in Sociology from the University of Buea in Cameroon, a Master's degree in Earth Science from the University of Yaounde in Cameroon, and a Doctorate in Geosciences from the University of Texas at Dallas. In addition to being a geoscientist with extensive experience in the oil and gas industry, he is a teacher and an entrepreneur.

Currently, he teaches at Missional University, Embry Riddle, and West Hills College. He is also the President of IEM Approach, a premier personal growth and leadership development company based on the infinite wisdom revealed over the ages. On a mission to inspire, equip, and motivate people from all walks of life to find their God-given purpose, pursue, and possess it. He is married and has five children.

If you want to invite Dr. Tangumonkem to come and speak at your event, please call 317-975-0806 or email eternalkingdom101@gmail.com.

Other Resources by the Author

Why I Refused to Become an Illegal Alien: Navigating the Complexities of the American Immigration System

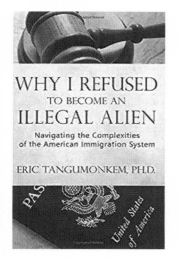

When it comes to the problem of illegal immigration, divisive rhetoric has shut out the voice of reason and common sense. Polarization has resulted in two extreme views--either open the borders wide and allow the free movement of people and goods, or close the borders and prevent people from coming in. The solution is somewhere in the middle . . . if we are willing to listen to one another. Why I Refused to Become an Illegal Alien chronicles the long and arduous journey of one man who immigrated legally and believes that the cost of allowing America's present immigration crisis to remain unresolved is too high. Drawing upon his deep Judeo-Christian roots, this newly-naturalized US citizen sets forth Bible-based solutions that emphasize the need to be our brother's keeper--to show love, mercy, and compassion and at the same time be fair and just.

Make Yourself at Home: An Immigrant's Guide to Settling in America

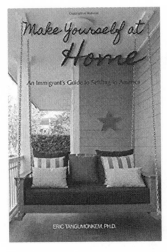

We live in a fallen world plagued by political unrest, conflicts, and wars. These factors, coupled with the desire for a better life, compel people to move to other areas—even across continents and oceans. Immigration brings people face to face with diverse cultures, and wherever diverse cultures meet, either there is immense personal growth, or things can go south quickly. The strategies introduced in this book are for immigrants who are new to the United States of America, but they are applicable to anyone who migrates within or outside of a country. Make Yourself at Home is a valuable resource for helping immigrants avoid the pitfalls experienced by those who have gone before them. Author Eric Tangumonkem, himself an immigrant and naturalized American citizen, presents practical assimilation strategies for education, money, home life, community, and health that, if followed, will position immigrants to excel in their new home.

Coming to America: A Journey of Faith

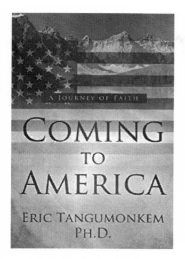

Do you struggle with trusting God with your finances? Feel that God is calling you to do something big but you can't see how it will be accomplished? Fear that He has abandoned you after starting your journey of faith? Coming to America: A Journey of Faith is Eric Tangumonkem's story of wrestling with these thoughts and doubts. God called him to America from Cameroon to pursue graduate studies at the University of Texas at Dallas, but he had no money to put towards this dream. In this book, Tangumonkem shares his journey of learning to trust God as he stepped out in faith and came to America despite a lack of funds. He also shares some of his formative experiences prior to this call-experiences that will encourage readers in their faith. Tangumonkem's life is a testimony to the faithfulness of God, and he is careful to give Him all of the glory.

The Use and Abuse of Titles in the Church

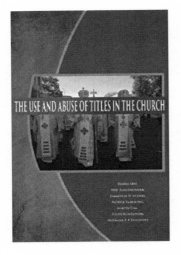

This book examines reasons behind the disturbing proliferation of titles in Christendom in recent times by seven distinguished Christian professionals. The book challenges readers to stay on the straight and narrow road, which celebrates ministers with titles bestowed based on sound Biblical foundations, while shunning those with titles associated with self-promotion and doctrinal errors. The book also provides the following actionable insights: · How to identify the proper use of titles A history on the use of titles in Christendom How to avoid the pitfalls of acquiring bogus titles An understanding of the relationship between titles and leadership.

Seven Success Keys Learned From My Father

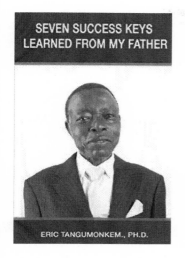

This is a book about my father, my teacher, my role model and hero. A man of passion like any other man, but a man of exceptional qualities and abilities as well. The following are the seven keys to success my father passed to me: Fear of God, Humility, Education, Integrity, Hard work, Prayer and Vision. All these keys have been instrumental in making me who I am today. In addition to these keys, my father was present when we were growing up. He made it a point of duty to talk the talk and walk the walk before us. This book illustrates how these seven keys to success were interwoven in our day-to-day lives and how they have opened unprecedented doors of success to me. My sincere prayer for you as you read this book is that these keys will open all doors for you and bring the success you desire so strongly. Amen!

Viajando a America: Un Camino de Fe (Spanish Edition)

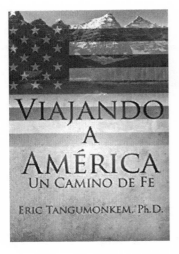

¿Lucha con confiar en Dios con sus finanzas? Siente que Dios le está llamando a hacer algo grande, pero usted no puede ver la forma en que se llevará a cabo? ¿Teme a que Él le ha abandonado después de comenzar su camino de fe?

Viajando a América: Un Camino de Fe es la historia de Eric Tangumonkem, de su lucha con estos pensamientos y dudas. Dios lo llamó a América desde Camerún para realizar estudios de posgrado en la Universidad de Texas en Dallas, pero no tenía dinero para seguir este llamado. En este libro, Tangumonkem comparte su viaje de aprender a confiar en Dios cuando caminó en la fe y llegó a Estados Unidos a pesar de su falta de fondos. También comparte algunas de sus experiencias formativas previas a esta convocatoria-experiencias que estimularán a los lectores en su fe. La vida de Tangumonkem es un testimonio de la fidelidad de Dios, y él tiene cuidado en darle toda la.

Mon Odysee Americaine: Une Experience De Foi

As-tu du mal à confier tes soucis financiers au Seigneur? Ressens-tu que Dieu t'appelle à faire quelque chose de grand, mais tu ne sais comment cela va se réaliser? Crains-tu qu'il va t'abandonner en chemin? Mon Odyssée Américaine: une expérience de foi est l'histoire d'Éric Tangumonkem et de sa lutte contre le doute et les pensées susmentionnées. Dieu l'a appelé depuis le Cameroun pour aller poursuivre ses études supérieures à l'Université du Texas à Dallas, mais il n'avait pas d'argent pour réaliser ce rêve. Dans ce livre, le Dr Tangumonkem partage avec vous les péripéties de son voyage qui l'ont amené à faire davantage confiance à Dieu alors qu'il se rendit aux États-Unis par la foi. Il partage également certaines des expériences qui l'ont bâti avant même son appel —expériences qui vont encourager les lecteurs dans leur foi. La vie du Dr Tangumonkem est un témoignage de la fidélité de Dieu à qui il rend toute la gloire.

God's Supernatural Agenda: 7 Secrets to Lasting Wealth and Prosperity

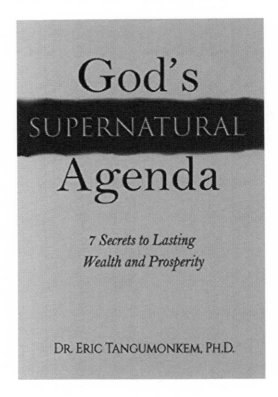

IEM PRESS

To order additional copies of this book, call 317-975-0806 or visit www.iempublishing.com for more information on other quality custom-published books.

"Inspiring, equipping, and motivating one author at a time."

Made in the USA
Monee, IL
21 February 2020

22102062R00081